HEATH
MIDDLELEVEL
LITERATURE

W9-BQS-550

Adventures and Adventurers

▼ THEME ▼
CHALLENGES AND ACHIEVEMENTS

A U T H O R S

Donna Alvermann
Linda Miller Cleary
Kenneth Donelson
Donald Gallo
Alice Haskins
J. Howard Johnston
John Lounsbury
Alleen Pace Nilsen
Robert Pavlik
Jewell Parker Rhodes
Alberto Alvaro Ríos
Sandra Schurr
Lyndon Searfoss
Julia Thomason
Max Thompson
Carl Zon

D.C. Heath and Company
Lexington, Massachusetts / Toronto, Ontario
HEATH

STAFF CREDITS

EDITORIAL — Barbara A. Brennan, Helen Byers, Christopher Johnson, Kathleen Kennedy Kelley, Owen Shows, Rita M. Sullivan
Proofreading: JoAnne B. Sgroi

CONTRIBUTING WRITERS — Nance Davidson, Florence Harris

SERIES DESIGN — Robin Herr

BOOK DESIGN — Caroline Bowden, Daniel Derdula, Susan Geer, Diana Maloney, Angela Sciaraffa, Bonnie Chayes Yousefian
Art Editing: Carolyn Langley

PHOTOGRAPHY — *Series Photography Coordinator*: Carmen Johnson
Photo Research Supervisor: Martha Friedman
Photo Researchers: Wendy Enright, Linda Finigan, Po-yee McKenna, PhotoSearch, Inc., Gillian Speeth, Denise Theodores
Assignment Photography Coordinators: Susan Doheny, Gayna Hoffman, Shawna Johnston

COMPUTER PREPRESS — Ricki Pappo, Kathy Meisl
Richard Curran, Michele Locatelli

PERMISSIONS — Dorothy B. McLeod

PRODUCTION — Patrick Connolly

Cover Photograph: © Zefa/Josef Mallaun, The Stock Market. **Cover Design:** Steve Snider

Copyright © 1995 by D.C. Heath and Company, a division of Houghton Mifflin Company

Acknowledgments for copyrighted material are on page 125 and constitute an extension of this page.

Published simultaneously in Canada

Printed in the United States of America

International Standard Book Number: 0-669-32104-4 (soft cover)
10 11 12-RRD-06 05 04

International Standard Book Number: 0-669-38173-X (hard cover)
4 5 6 7 8 9 10-RRD-99 98 97

Middle Level Authors

Donna Alvermann, University of Georgia
Alice Haskins, Howard County Public Schools, Maryland
J. Howard Johnston, University of South Florida
John Lounsbury, Georgia College
Sandra Schurr, University of South Florida
Julia Thomason, Appalachian State University
Max Thompson, Appalachian State University
Carl Zon, California Assessment Collaborative

Literature and Language Arts Authors

Linda Miller Cleary, University of Minnesota
Kenneth Donelson, Arizona State University
Donald Gallo, Central Connecticut State University
Alleen Pace Nilsen, Arizona State University
Robert Pavlik, Cardinal Stritch College, Milwaukee
Jewell Parker Rhodes, Arizona State University
Alberto Alvaro Ríos, Arizona State University
Lyndon Searfoss, Arizona State University

Teacher Consultants

Suzanne Aubin, Patapsco Middle School, Ellicott City, Maryland
Judy Baxter, Newport News Public Schools, Newport News, Virginia
Saundra Bryn, Director of Research and Development, El Mirage, Arizona
Lorraine Gerhart, Elmbrook Middle School, Elm Grove, Wisconsin
Kathy Tuchman Glass, Burlingame Intermediate School, Burlingame, California
Lisa Mandelbaum, Crocker Middle School, Hillsborough, California
Lucretia Pannozzo, John Jay Middle School, Katonah, New York
Carol Schultz, Jerling Junior High, Orland Park, Illinois
Jeanne Siebenman, Grand Canyon University, Phoenix, Arizona
Gail Thompson, Garey High School, Pomona, California
Rufus Thompson, Grace Yokley School, Ontario, California
Tom Tufts, Conniston Middle School, West Palm Beach, Florida
Edna Turner, Harpers Choice Middle School, Columbia, Maryland
C. Anne Webb, Buerkle Junior High School, St. Louis, Missouri
Geri Yaccino, Thompson Junior High School, St. Charles, Illinois

CONTENTS

Knight with maiden German, 14th century, illuminated manuscript

Contents **5**

ASKING BIG QUESTIONS ABOUT THE LITERATURE

PROJECTS

1 WRITING WORKSHOP

WRITING A TRAVEL BROCHURE 106-111

Have you ever dreamed of wild and exotic places? Let this project take you there!

2 COOPERATIVE LEARNING

PLANNING A TREASURE HUNT 112-113

Plan a treasure hunt with a trail of clues leading to a hidden treasure.

3 HELPING YOUR COMMUNITY

CELEBRATING LOCAL ADVENTURERS 114-115

Work with a partner or group to put together a tribute to the adventurers in your community.

ADVENTURE

MAZE

*A*fter reading a thrilling adventure story, does your imagination sweep you into your own adventures? You can use some of those imaginings to plan a daring journey that challenges the traveler at every turn. Look at this maze. Can you find the way to the center? Create a similar Adventure Maze on paper and watch a classmate find a way through it.

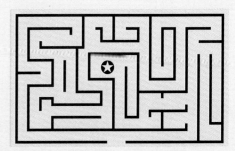

Build **1** an adventure.

Finding a path through a maze can be an adventure, but it's not enough of a challenge for your travelers. You'll need to provide some surprises along the way. Alone or with a group, brainstorm challenging obstacles that a daring traveler might face. What kind of surprises do travelers encounter in TV and movie adventures? Do they encounter volcanoes? Earthquakes? A tunnel of snakes? Make a list of obstacles and challenges that you could build into your maze.

Put it all together.

Now design your maze. Follow these steps.

1. Draw a large square or circle and divide it into equal parts.
2. Draw a path through the parts. Then add twists, turns, and dead ends.
3. Add obstacles at the twists and turns. Force the traveler to choose between dangers.

When you're satisfied, copy the maze neatly. Decorate it too.

Enjoy your adventure.

Ask a classmate to travel through the maze, explaining his or her decisions. Watch and listen. What challenges does the traveler avoid, face, dread, enjoy? Why?

In your journal, write about your own adventure in planning the maze. What was a challenge, and what was exciting? You may find that creating an adventure can be an adventure in itself.

Asking Big Questions About the Theme

? What makes an adventure?

What stories, movies, TV shows, and experiences come to mind when you think of the word *adventure*? What features do all adventures share? In a small group, discuss these questions. Then create an exciting adventure. Write the first paragraph of an adventure story on a sheet of paper. Take turns adding paragraphs to the story. Allow each person just one minute of writing time.

Share the adventure with other groups or the class. Discuss which are the best adventures and why.

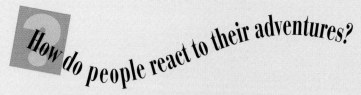

? How do people react to their adventures?

Imagine that you and a friend have just been shipwrecked on a tropical island. How do you feel? Would you be frightened or would you see your adventure as an exciting challenge? Act out the scene with a partner. Then perform your scene for classmates and watch their performances. Compare your reactions to their reactions by making a diagram like the one below.

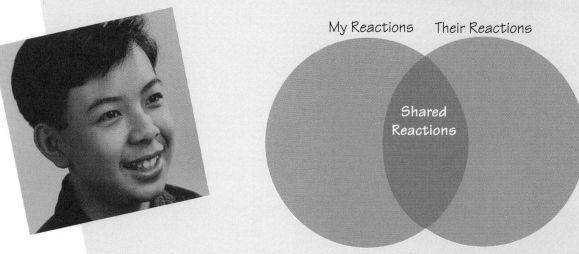

My Reactions   Their Reactions

Shared Reactions

What are adventurers like?

Someone's in danger on Menace Mountain, and a daring adventurer is needed to come to the rescue! Write a want ad for an adventurer. Work with a partner or group to decide what qualities to ask for in the ad. First, discuss the qualities of some real or fictional adventurers. Then, in your journal, make a Word Map like the one below. List words, phrases, actions that the word *adventurer* brings to mind. Finally write an ad for an adventurer.

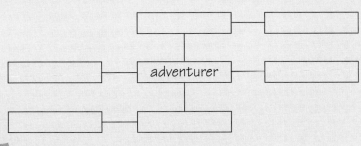

How are you an adventurer?

In your journal, write a response to this final Big Question. Use some of the sentence starters below to get your ideas going.

- My biggest (strangest, funniest, most exciting) adventure was . . .
- I am an adventurer because . . .
- Things I find exciting are . . .
- When faced with a challenge, I feel . . .

NOW

Think!

With a partner or group, brainstorm additional questions about adventures. Write the questions in your journal. As you work through this unit, keep asking the four Big Questions and your own questions too. How do your responses change as you read the literature in this unit?

Portrait of Annie Peck

Friday, August 28–
Saturday, September 5, 1908
Yungay, Peru

Annie Smith Peck pushed open the shutters and leaned out the window. She looked past the square in Yungay's[1] center, down a narrow dirt road lined by red-roofed houses, past the fields of wheat and corn, up to the snow-capped twin peaks of Huascarán,[2] the highest mountain in Peru. It was a maze of snow and

1. **Yungay** [yün′ gī]
2. **Huascarán** [wäs kä rän′]

DOREEN RAPPAPORT

ice at over 22,000 feet (6,700 meters) above sea level. No one had ever climbed it to the top.

Huascarán is shaped like a horse's saddle. Thousands of feet of rocky slopes lead to an immense glacier that spans the twin peaks. The glacier is a moving mass of ice. Anyone climbing it may encounter dangerous crevasses—deep fissures[3] that drop suddenly into abysses[4]—and snow avalanches that unexpectedly thunder down.

Climate is another danger. Ice-cold winds batter the mountain.

3. **fissures** [fish′ ərz]: long, narrow splits.
4. **abysses** [ə bis′ əz]: deep openings in the earth.

At such high altitudes there is less oxygen to breathe. The body's metabolism[5] slows down. Every step tests a person's physical endurance to its limits. No wonder no one had ever reached the top.

In the last four years Annie had tried five times to scale these snowy peaks and icy crags, and five times she had failed. Her last attempt had been only ten days ago.

People constantly asked her why she pursued this dangerous, impossible dream. Annie didn't try to make them understand. She didn't think that people who viewed mountains from valleys or from railroad trains could ever understand the beauty and power of those white-domed peaks floating toward the deep blue of the sky, belonging more to heaven than to earth.

But it wasn't only the beauty of mountains that attracted Annie. Ever since childhood Annie had taken on challenges. As the youngest child and only girl among three brothers, she had learned not to be intimidated by men's supposedly superior physical strength and endurance. When her brothers refused to let her join them in their games, she practiced until she was as good as they were, if not better. When her brothers went off to college, Annie vowed she would go too, even though there were only a few women's colleges and fewer coed colleges at that time. In 1874 she gained admission to the University of Michigan. She majored in Greek and excelled in every subject she studied. But earning a college degree wasn't enough for Annie. She went on to get a master's in Greek and became one of the first women college professors in the United States.

In 1885, on a trip through Switzerland, Annie saw the 14,690 foot (4,478 meter) Matterhorn, and her passion for the classics started to give way to a passion for mountain climbing. She became determined to scale its "frowning walls." She prepared by climbing smaller mountains in Greece and Switzerland. In 1888 she and her oldest brother scaled California's 14,162 foot (4,316 meter) Mount Shasta. In 1895 she became the third woman to conquer the Matterhorn.

5. **metabolism** [mə tabʹ ə lizʹ əm]: bodily processes that maintain life in a living being.

She became instantaneously famous. People marveled at the endurance and courage of this woman, forty-five years old and barely five feet tall. Her climbing outfit—a hip-length tunic,[6] short pants, high boots and a canvas hat tied with a veil under her chin—created as much of a sensation as her daring achievement. How unladylike, men said, and many women agreed. But Annie refused to wear floor-length skirts like other women climbers. It was ridiculous and dangerous to dress "like a lady."

Annie's triumph over the Matterhorn propelled her on. She gave up teaching and became a full-time climber, supporting herself by lecturing about her adventures. By 1900, having achieved over twenty successful climbs, she was recognized as one of the world's foremost climbers in a field still considered a man's sport.

But that wasn't enough for Annie either. She became determined to conquer a mountain no man had ever conquered. That mountain was Huascarán.

Annie closed the shutters, picked up her clothing sack and a heavy wool poncho and went downstairs. The four porters were carrying the expedition equipment outside. One sack held the ice axes, climbing irons, poles and ropes. Annie's lightweight silk tent and the sleeping bags were rolled up in the corner. The kerosene stove and kettles filled a third sack. Food was in a fourth bag. In a fifth bag were Annie's camera and a hypsometer, which she would use to measure the altitude at the top of Huascarán to establish its exact height.

Annie gave her clothing and poncho to one of the men. As temperatures dropped on the climb, she would eventually wear everything in the sack: two woolen face masks, fur mittens, black woolen sleeves, three suits of lightweight wool underwear, two pairs of tights, two pairs of woolen stockings, knickers,[7] two flannel shirts, a jacket and two sweaters. Her hiking boots were big and clumsy. They had to be four sizes larger than her regular shoes to accommodate the heavy stockings.

6. **tunic** [tü′ nik]: a long shirt.
7. **knickers** [nik′ ərz]: short, loose trousers gathered at the knee.

Unfortunately none of her clothing was water- or windproof. Admiral Peary,[8] the famous Arctic explorer, had lent her a waterproof Eskimo suit, but on her last climb it had fallen irretrievably out of a porter's hands into a crevasse.

She went outside. Her guides, Gabriel Zumtaugwald and Rudolf Taugwalder, were supervising the packing of supplies on the horses. Like other expert climbers, Annie favored Swiss guides. They knew so much about snow and rock that they always chose the most practical and safe paths even when in unfamiliar territory.

Gabriel and Rudolf were skilled but stubborn, and impatient whenever Annie made suggestions—even though she was their employer and knew the mountain better than they did. They wouldn't listen when she suggested they wear at least two pairs of wool stockings. Her guides of two years ago, wearing two pairs of stockings, had barely escaped losing their toes to frostbite. They didn't like taking advice from a woman.

The party set off on horseback for the three-hour ride to the copper mines, where they would rest overnight before hiking to the snow line. The horses trotted down the narrow walled road out of the village and soon ascended to where the houses became more scattered. The air was fragrant with blossoms of yellow broom and blue larkspur. Fields of wheat and corn blanketed the landscape with deep yellows. On the mountain snow was falling. An occasional villager, bent from years of working in the fields, passed them on the road.

When they arrived at the mines, Annie felt faint and a bit sick. She didn't know why. The ride had been easy enough. She ate a small bowl of soup and two boiled eggs and lay down to take a nap. But sleep did not come easily.

When Annie saw clouds over the mountain the next morning, she postponed the ascent. The fresh snow needed at least another day of melting by the sun and freezing at night to make the mountain suitable for climbing.

8. **Admiral Peary** [pir′ ē]: United States naval officer who discovered the North Pole in 1909.

Saddle and north peak of Huascarán

At eight A.M. the next day they set out for the snow line. The walking was easy. Within six hours, they reached the first campsite, set up their tents, had soup and tea, and went to bed at sunset.

By seven the following morning they were at the glacier. The porters put climbing irons over their shoes to bite into the surface of snow and ice. Annie and the guides wore boots studded with nails. Annie's studs weren't as pointed as her guides', but she didn't want to wear climbing irons. On the last ascent the strap on one of Annie's irons had been too tight. It had hindered her circulation. Two of her toes and the top of her right foot had gotten slightly frostbitten.

The climbing continued to be easy. Annie's instinct to wait the extra day had been right. The snow was easy to walk on. In seven hours they were well up in the saddle of the mountain. They pitched their tent under a snow wall. But despite the wall's shelter, a chilling wind swept through the tent all night.

There was no wind the next morning, but the air was thin and bitter cold. Annie thought it was the coldest day she had ever experienced on the mountain in all her climbs.

The ascent became radically steeper. Gabriel went first, probing for crevasses with his pickaxe and cutting small zigzag steps up the almost perpendicular[9] wall. Annie, tied to a rope with Rudolf and a porter named Lucas, followed, pushing her pole into the glassy surface. The pole's pointed iron provided leverage,[10] but the climbing was difficult and exhausting.

An hour later they reached a bridge of ice over a crevasse. Annie hesitated to cross it because there was no way to tell how strong it was. Rudolf crawled quickly over it on his hands and knees, then sat on the other side and wound the rope, still tied to Annie and the porter, around his ice axe to anchor it. Annie hurried across next, then knotted her length of rope around her ice axe. Lucas was carrying too much on his back to hurry across. He stepped cautiously onto the ice bridge and suddenly slipped off the bridge and disappeared into the crevasse. Annie heard his cry as she gripped the rope more firmly to keep from being pulled over with him.

"Quick, quick." Gabriel, tied to the other three porters on a second rope, motioned for the porters to untie themselves. He threw their rope down to Lucas, who—though hanging head down—managed to tie it to his own rope and miraculously turn himself upright. He tugged on the rope. Annie and the men pulled him up. Annie was relieved to see him, but was dismayed to see that his

9. **perpendicular** [pėr′ pən dik′ yə lər]: very steep, vertical.
10. **leverage** [lev′ ər ij]: increased ability to climb.

pack, with the new stove in it, was not with him. They couldn't go on without the stove.

"I'll go down for it," Gabriel said, and within seconds he was lowered down on a rope. Annie was worried. They were at least 19,000 feet above sea level. Exerting oneself at this height was dangerous. And maybe it was a fool's errand. There was no telling how deep the crevasse was or if Gabriel could even find the pack.

She waited impatiently. Ten minutes later Gabriel pulled on the rope. They hauled him up. The pack, with the stove in it, was in his hands.

They moved on. By dark they were at the top of the saddle. Tomorrow, with any luck, she would reach the top. *Finally, after all these years.*

Winds battered the tent all night and were so fierce the next morning that Annie suggested postponing the final climb until the wind died down.

"It's too dangerous," she said, "and we need rest." She was exhausted from the last two days and knew that the men had to be too, even though they wouldn't admit it.

"It'll be less windy higher up," countered Rudolf.

"I know this mountain," Annie argued. "Unless the wind dies down altogether, it'll be worse higher up."

"I think Rudolf's right," said Gabriel. "We should go on."

Annie yielded reluctantly. They agreed to leave the porters behind.

She was wearing every stitch of clothing she had packed but the poncho. She didn't want to put it on yet. It was too clumsy. She slipped a mask over her face and neck and put on her fur mittens. Rudolf put on his face mask. Gabriel didn't have a mask. Annie offered him her extra one and was surprised when he graciously accepted it.

"Could one of you carry my poncho?" This was asking a big favor, for at this altitude every extra bit of weight was a strain.

Rudolf acted as if he didn't hear her. "I'll do it," said Gabriel, even though he was already burdened with the food sack and the bag with hypsometer and camera.

Within an hour of climbing the sun was higher in the sky and Annie's hands were sweating inside the fur mittens. She took off her fur mittens and exchanged them for two pairs of woolen mittens in Rudolf's sack. One pair did not cover the fingers.

Up, up, the climbing was slow and strenuous. The cold winds had blown away the lighter snow on the surface, and the glacier was like glass.

"I've never seen such large patches of ice on any mountain in Switzerland," Rudolf said.

"I told you Huascarán is the fiercest mountain in the world," Annie said proudly.

They turned a ridge, and the wind knifed through Annie. She took her poncho from Gabriel. She needed her fur mittens. They stopped, and Rudolf opened his sack.

"Which ones first?" he asked, tucking Annie's wool sleeves and fur mittens under his right arm.

Hold on to them tight, Annie thought, but she didn't say it.

"The sleeves."

Rudolf reached under his arm, but the wind got there first. Annie watched a fur mitten blow over the precipice.[11] She was furious. There was no way to retrieve it. The woolen gloves would never be warm enough, and now her hands would probably get frostbitten.

Rudolf apologized. Annie ignored the apology. She hastily put the one fur mitten on over the other gloves on her right hand, which carried her pickaxe. It was more exposed to the cold than the left hand.

Up, up. The air was so thin, Annie had trouble breathing. It became harder and harder to move her legs. It was even hard pushing the pickaxe into the icy surface.

They stopped to eat. The meat and bread had frozen in the sack, but it didn't matter. They were too tired to eat much anyway. They nibbled on chocolate and raisins and drank the partially frozen tea in Rudolf's canteen.

"I'm too tired to go any farther," Rudolf announced.

Annie didn't want to stop. They were probably only an hour

11. **precipice** [pres′ ə pis]: very steep, almost vertical mountainside.

Highest camp, east side of Huascarán

away from the top. *So close now!* "You can rest and we'll go ahead," she said to Rudolf.

"No, let's all rest for an hour and then go on," said Gabriel. Annie agreed reluctantly.

The hour's rest did little to revive them. When they started climbing again, the cold, thin air was so debilitating[12] that they had to stop frequently.

At three P.M. they rounded the final rise leading to the top of the mountain. The wind was stronger than ever. Annie's left hand felt numb. She pulled off her mitten and saw that the hand was nearly black. She rubbed her fingers vigorously with snow to revive the circulation. The rubbing made her fingers ache, a good sign that

12. **debilitating** [di bil′ ə tāt ing]: causing to become weak.

they weren't frostbitten. She tucked her hands inside the poncho, grateful for its length.

"We'd better measure the altitude now," said Gabriel. "It may be too windy at the top."

They untied themselves from each other. Rudolf wandered off, but Annie paid no attention. She was too busy shielding the hypsometer from the wind as Gabriel struck one match after another, hoping to light the candles so they could boil the water. A hypsometer is an instrument that is able to determine altitude in relation to the boiling point of water, which decreases as altitude increases. Annie wanted to know exactly how high she was and whether she had set a world's record.

She looked around for Rudolf. *Where is he? Maybe if he helped, we could get the candles lit.* After twenty tries, they gave up. Annie was disappointed. Now she could only estimate how high the mountain really was.

"We'd better move on to the top. It's half past three," said Gabriel.

Annie looked around for Rudolf again.

Suddenly he appeared. "I've been to the top," he said.

How dare he steal the honor? He wouldn't have dared do this if I were a man. Just an hour ago he wanted to quit. And he hasn't done half as much work as Gabriel. The guides knew she expected, as was the tradition, that as organizer of the expedition she would be the first to place her foot on the top of the mountain.

I won't tell him now how mad I am, but if we get down alive, I'll tell him. If we get down alive . . . The thought frightened her.

She set out for the top without a word. The winds battered her, and several times she had to stop and lean on her pickaxe to catch her breath.

"Don't go too near the edge," warned Gabriel, stepping aside to let her arrive first on the top of the mountain.

I'm here after all these years. She wanted to shout for joy, but there was no time to waste. Soon it would be dark. It had taken seven hours to climb to the top. How long would it take to go down? Steep rocks and icy slopes were far more dangerous to descend than to climb. She hurriedly photographed the views on all sides.

They tied themselves together again. Rudolf led, cutting the steps. Annie was in the middle, Gabriel at the rear. Their lives depended on Gabriel. If they slipped and he couldn't hold the rope to stop their fall, all three could plunge to death.

They turned a ridge and confronted a sixty-degree slope. "Be careful," said Gabriel.

Something black flew by.

"What is it?" Annie cried.

"One of my mittens," said Rudolf. "I took it off to fasten my shoe."

Rudolf worked fast, cutting the steps the size of toeholds. Small steps were fine going up, but dangerous going down. Annie zigzagged her way down the steep slope. There was nothing to hold on to. She wished she had her climbing irons now. She needed that kind of grip on this glassy surface.

She missed a step and slid three feet. Gabriel's strong hands held the rope tightly, and she regained her footing. A few seconds later she missed another step and slipped again. She was about to yell, "It's not serious," when she slid again. Five, ten, fifteen feet down the incline. Again Gabriel's strong hands checked her fall.

Studio photograph of Annie Peck on the summit of Huascarán

"Get up," he yelled, but the rope was twisted so tightly around her waist that she couldn't move. The men came to her and hauled her up.

They moved on. Her poncho, swaying wide in the wind, constantly hid her view of her next step. Down, down she stepped. Again she slipped. Her fall pulled Rudolf down, too. Gabriel's strong hands checked both their falls.

I don't think we'll make it down alive. It's too dark and too slippery. And I'm so tired.

She slid again and again. She tried to convince herself that they would make it down alive.

She lost track of how much time was passing as she concentrated on each step. She wasn't even aware, three hours later, that they were on the gentler slope just over the campsite until Gabriel shouted, "We're safe. Now you can slide if you like."

Annie laughed. They untied themselves from each other and dragged their tired bodies toward the tent. It was half past ten. They were too tired to eat and almost too tired to lie down. But safety felt good.

In the tent Annie noticed both of Rudolf's hands were black. "Rub them hard," she said. But Rudolf was so weak, he couldn't do it. *I'll do it,* thought Annie, but she was too tired to do it. *I'll get a porter to do it.* But in her tiredness, she forgot.

The three climbers huddled together on one side of the tent across from the porters. Annie wrapped the blankets around herself and the two men. When she realized the middle was the warmest spot, she moved to the outside and let Rudolf be in the center.

When they awakened the next morning, the wind was fierce. They were too exhausted to complete the rest of the trip down the mountain. By Thursday the wind had abated,[13] and feeling more rested, they started down the mountain. They arrived at the mine two days later, on Saturday morning, September 5, about 10 A.M. After breakfast, they returned to Yungay.

Becoming the first person to climb to the top of Huascarán brought Annie world fame. The Peruvian government gave her a gold medal. In

---

13. **abated** [ə bāt′ əd]: lessened in force.

1928 the Lima Geographical Society named the north peak of Huascarán Ana Peck. But Annie's triumph over Huascarán was marred for her by the subsequent[14] amputation of Rudolf's left hand, a finger of his right hand and half of one foot.

Because the hypsometer had not worked, Annie could only estimate Huascarán's height. At the saddle she and her guides had measured the altitude at 20,000 feet (6,100 meters). Based on this figure, they estimated that the north and south peaks were at least 23,000 feet (7,000 meters), making Huascarán the highest mountain in Peru and the highest mountain ever scaled by a man or woman.

Fanny Bullock Workman, up to this time the world's highest woman climber, challenged Annie's estimate of Huascarán. Bullock Workman sent a team of scientists to Yungay to measure Huascarán by triangulation: This method uses trigonometry to measure height. Bullock Workman's team concluded that the north and south peaks were no more than 21,812 feet (6,648 meters) and 22,187 feet (6,763 meters) respectively.

Annie eventually conceded that Huascarán was "not so lofty" as she had hoped. Bullock Workman still held the world's altitude record for a woman climber, but Annie had succeeded in climbing a mountain that no man or woman had ever climbed. Annie continued climbing until she was eighty-two years old.

14. **subsequent** [sub′ sə kwənt]: following or happening next.

DOREEN RAPPAPORT

Doreen Rappaport lives in New York City and is the author of several books for young people. Rappaport has also worked on educational programs in American history, literature, and music. The selection you've just read is from *Living Dangerously: American Women Who Risked Their Lives for Adventure*. She has also edited a collection of short autobiographies called *American Women: Their Lives in Their Words*. Rappaport's other books are *The Boston Coffee Party*, *Escape from Slavery*, and *Trouble at the Mines*.

BURNING

GARY SNYDER

JOHN MUIR ON MT. RITTER:

After scanning its face again and again,
I began to scale it, picking my holds
With intense caution. About half-way
To the top, I was suddenly brought to
A dead stop, with arms outspread   5
Clinging close to the face of the rock
Unable to move hand or foot
Either up or down. My doom
Appeared fixed. I MUST fall.
There would be a moment of   10
Bewilderment, and then,
A lifeless rumble down the cliff
To the glacier below.
My mind seemed to fill with a
Stifling smoke. This terrible eclipse   15
Lasted only a moment, when life blazed
Forth again with preternatural[1] clearness.
I seemed suddenly to become possessed
Of a new sense. My trembling muscles
Became firm again, every rift and flaw in   20
The rock was seen as through a microscope,
My limbs moved with a positiveness and precision
With which I seemed to have
Nothing at all to do.

---

1. **preternatural** [prē′ tər nach′ ər əl]: something above or beyond
nature.

GARY SNYDER

Gary Snyder was born in 1930 in San Francisco. As a young boy growing up in California, Oregon, and Washington, Snyder loved the wilderness and was upset by the destruction of the Pacific Northwest forests. He began to study how Native American cultures live in harmony with nature. As he grew older, Snyder became an expert mountain climber. He worked as a seaman, logger, trail crew member, and forest lookout.

Asian art and Buddhism interested Snyder as well. Many of his poems draw on ancient chants and songs from both Asian and Native American cultures. The poem you've just read is the eighth segment of a long poem sequence called "Burning."

Le Grotte Vecchie (or Untitled)
Michael Goldberg, 1981, powders, pastels, and chalk on canvas, 108 $^1/_4$" x 87"

The Stars, My Goal: Guion Stewart Bluford, Jr.

JIM HASKINS

As the twentieth century progressed, humankind turned its eyes to the unexplored expanse of outer space. While small discoveries were continually being made about our home planet, the earth, the frontier to be explored now stretched beyond the planet and spread to the stars. The 1960s saw years of effort to break the bonds of gravity, effort that had begun with the launching of *Sputnik I* [1] by the Soviet Union in 1957. Inspired by that launching and the concomitant interest in a space program in the United States, a young black high school student, Guion Stewart (Guy) Bluford, Jr., also turned his eyes to the stars.

Guy Bluford was born on November 22, 1942, in Philadelphia, Pennsylvania. His mother was a teacher of special education and his father a mechanical engineer.

1. *Sputnik I* [sput′ nik]: first satellite put into space by the former Soviet Union in 1957.

Even as a baby Guy took after his father, showing an interest in mechanical things. He wanted to know how they worked. Guy had lots of mechanical toys to take apart, . . . but what he liked best were things that flew.

That interest was to fill his childhood. His room was filled with airplane models and pictures of airplanes. His interest wasn't so much in flying them, but in designing them. He was fascinated with the way they were put together, why they flew. His father encouraged this curiosity and made his many engineering books available to Guy. Guy knew very early that he wanted to be an aerospace engineer. Guy knew he wanted to design, build, and fly spacecraft, and when he was fifteen and *Sputnik I* was launched, his dreams became even more real.

In the late 1950s, just as the days of the civil rights movement[2] were beginning, the idea of a black man becoming an aerospace engineer was barely conceivable[3] to many people. Although encouraged at home, Guy didn't receive that same encouragement at school. His high school guidance counselor didn't urge him to pursue his goal and go to college; in fact, he was told that he wasn't college material. He was told that he should aim for a technical school or learn a mechanical trade. However, he says,

I really wasn't too concerned about what that counselor said. I just ignored it. I'm pretty sure that all of us have had times when somebody told us we couldn't do this or shouldn't do that. I had such a strong interest in aerospace engineering by then that nothing a counselor said was going to stop me.

2. **civil rights movement:** movement that aimed to assure that every United States citizen, regardless of race or sex, has the rights guaranteed by the Constitution.
3. **conceivable** [kən sēʹ və bəl]: possible to imagine.

In the fall of 1960, Guy started college at Pennsylvania State University, in the aerospace engineering program. In addition to his regular studies, Guy also joined the air force Reserve Officers Training Corps (ROTC), hoping to become a pilot. In his junior year, however, he failed a physical and couldn't qualify as a pilot. During ROTC summer camp that year, he at least passed the flight physical—and got his first ride in an air force T-33 plane. "I changed directions right then and there," he said. "I decided to go into the Air Force as a pilot. I thought that if I were a pilot, I would be a better engineer." During his senior year at Penn State, Guy flew as a pilot in the air force ROTC and, upon graduation, received the ROTC's Distinguished Graduate Award.

While at Penn State, Guy had met and married Linda Tull, a fellow student; after graduation he joined the air force, moving to Arizona with his wife and new son, Guion III, who had been born in June of 1964. His second son, James Trevor, was born in 1965 just at the time the Vietnam War was becoming an important factor in the lives of many Americans.

For the next several years, Guy saw little of his family. As pilot of an F-4C fighter plane, he was assigned to the 557th Tactical Fighter Squadron, based in Cam Ranh Bay,[4] South Vietnam. During his tour of duty he flew 144 combat missions and received ten air force medals. But he had not forgotten his goal of becoming an aerospace engineer and flying in outer space.

When Guy returned to the United States, he applied to the Air Force Institute of Technology, receiving a master's degree in 1974 and, in 1978, a Ph.D. in aerospace engineering. His doctoral thesis was entitled "A Numerical Solution of Supersonic and Hypersonic Viscous Flow Fields Around Thin Planar Delta Wings." As he explains:

Delta wings are triangular wings. I calculated how the air goes around the wings at speeds greater than the speed of sound—three to four times the

4. **Cam Ranh Bay** (käm rän bā]

speed of sound and faster. If you had picked a place anywhere along a wing, I could have told you what the pressure, the density, and the velocity of the air was above and below that place. I developed a computer program that could do that.

The same year Guy received his Ph.D., he applied to enter the astronaut training program at NASA (the National Aeronautics and Space Administration). NASA seemed, to Guy, to be the ideal place to put both his engineering and piloting skills to use, although he wasn't sure if he would be accepted. In 1978 alone, 8,878 other people had applied for the program. A few weeks later, however, he learned that he had been accepted. It was the fulfillment of a dream. Bluford and his family quickly moved to Houston, where he began his training.

The astronaut training program lasted a year and involved studying subjects such as shuttle systems, geology, medicine, aerodynamics,[5] communications, and astronomy. It also involved a great deal of travel.

Sputnik, 1957

We went to a lot of the NASA space centers, including Kennedy Space Center at Cape Canaveral, Florida; Marshall Space Center in Huntsville, Alabama, where they develop the engines; and Rockwell Aircraft Company on the West Coast, where they build the shuttles. We traveled around the country, meeting all of the people associated with the shuttle program.

5. **aerodynamics** [er′ ō dī nam′ iks]: branch of science that deals with pressure or resistance on flying bodies by air or other gases in motion.

By 1979, Guy Bluford was a full-fledged astronaut, qualified to go into space. He spent the next several years in further training, flying the "shuttle simulators" in both Houston and California, hoping and waiting, as were all the astronauts, to be chosen for that special ride beyond the skies of earth.

The shuttle program had begun in 1972, three years after Neil Armstrong and Edwin Aldrin had taken their historic walk on the moon. After the moon landing, interest in the space program had waned[6] somewhat. The 1970s were full of problems here on earth that diverted public interest: the Watergate scandals[7] of the Nixon administration, the Vietnam War,[8] and rising inflation[9] in the economy. One reason NASA began the shuttle program was to save money. The shuttle, unlike earlier rockets, was reusable. More versatile than the earlier rockets, it served not only as transportation, but also as a laboratory and living quarters. It could carry many things into space and was, compared to the rockets, much larger.

The first space shuttle, *Columbia*, was launched in April of 1981. The second shuttle, *Challenger*, went into service in 1983. On its second flight—two months before the flight Guy Bluford would be on—one of three mission specialists was Dr. Sally Ride, the first American woman in space.

Guy Bluford did not want to be known as merely a "black astronaut": he wanted to be known as a man who did a good job. All of the astronauts shared this view. As Sally Ride said about all the publicity her flight had generated, "I didn't go into the space program to make money or be famous." In 1983, when Guy was told that he was scheduled for the next *Challenger* flight, he was exhilarated—

6. **waned** [wānd]: lessened, grown smaller.
7. **Watergate scandals:** burglary of the Democratic Party Headquarters in 1972 at the Watergate buildings in Washington, D.C., and other illegal actions, resulting in the resignation of President Richard M. Nixon.
8. **Vietnam War** [vē et′ näm′]: war fought by South Vietnam, the United States, and their allies against the Vietcong (communist guerrillas), North Vietnam, and their allies from about 1957 to 1973.
9. **inflation** [in flā′ shən]: sharp increase in prices caused by the circulation of too much paper money or bank credit.

not to be the first black American in space, but because, finally, he would be doing what he had dreamed of all his life: putting *all* his skills to use.

On August 30, 1983, thunderstorms had swept across the sandy expanse of Cape Canaveral, Florida, but the air was now clear. In the hot, damp night, the *Challenger* stood over five stories high on launch pad 39-A. It was lighted both from above, by lights on the gantry,[10] and from below, as this would be the first nighttime launch since *Apollo 17* in 1972.

The five men inside the *Challenger* were busy checking equipment, listening to the hollow voice of mission control as the final countdown proceeded. Aboard were thirty-four-year-old Dale Gardner, a navy fighter pilot and engineer; Dr. William Thornton, at fifty-four the oldest person to fly in space; Richard Truly, a Vietnam War veteran and test pilot, who would serve as commander of the shuttle; thirty-nine-year-old Daniel Brandenstein, a navy commander; and Guion Bluford, Jr., who would serve as mission specialist. Guy was in charge of the experiments the crew were to conduct during the flight.

Just before lift-off, the crew received a message from President Ronald Reagan. "With this effort," he said, "we acknowledge proudly the first ascent of a black American into space." But Guy wasn't thinking of that; he was thinking of the flight. He was eager, curious, and excited, but not afraid: "We'd spent so much time training for the mission and riding in shuttle simulators[11] that we

Portrait of Guy Bluford

were pretty well prepared. It's like preparing for an exam. You study as much as you can, and the better prepared you are, the less frightened you are about taking the exam."

10. **gantry** [gan′ trē]: bridge-like framework for supporting the space shuttle while on the ground.
11. **simulators** [sim′ yə lāt ərz]: mock space shuttles that imitate a real journey into space to prepare the astronauts for the real thing.

At 2:32 A.M., August 30, 1983, fire blazed from the rockets and lit up the Florida landscape. As Richard Truly described it, "It got brighter and brighter. When the boosters separated it was 500 times brighter than I remember [from past launches]." Dale Gardner tried to twist around for a better view; "I damn near blinded myself," he said later. The brightness of the rockets' flare surprised all of the men.

"But otherwise, there weren't any surprises," Guy said. "What amazed me was that the shuttle flew just like the simulator said it was going to fly. The only differences were the motion, the vibration, and the noise. You don't get those in simulators. When I felt the movement and heard the noise, I thought, Hey, this thing really does take off and roar!"

Once in orbit, Bluford began to operate one of the main experiments, an electrophoresis[12] system designed to separate living cells, aimed at one day producing new medical advances. It was difficult, initially, to work in weightlessness, but also exhilarating. Although all the men had trained for weightlessness in a water-immersion tank,[13] it was still a new sensation. But everything was new and exciting. Circling the earth every ninety minutes, the crew slept, ate, and did their work in that new frontier—space.

On September 5, the shuttle glided to a perfect landing back on earth, at Edwards Air Force Base in California. Only later did NASA reveal that the crew had been in

12. **electrophoresis** [i lek′ trō fə rē′ sis]: movement of extremely small particles of matter influenced by an electric field.
13. **water-immersion tank** [i mėr′ zhən]: tank in which astronauts prepare for the weightlessness of space.

danger: The lining of a solid fuel booster's[14] nozzle had almost burned through during launching. Such an accident would have thrown the shuttle wildly off course, causing it to crash. Fourteen seconds—the time it would have taken for the lining to burn all the way through—was all that had separated the crew and shuttle from disaster.

All who venture to explore the unknown recognize the threat of disaster. This possibility doesn't stop them, however; risk is part of the job. So is determination. Throughout his life, Guion Bluford had one goal in mind—to work and fly in space, and he was determined to let nothing get in the way of achieving that goal. As he has said, it was "difficult at times—I had to struggle through those courses at Penn State—but if you really want to do something and are willing to put in the hard work it takes, then someday—bingo, you've done it!" With this kind of stick-to-itiveness, it isn't surprising that Guy Bluford became the first black American explorer of space.

14. **solid fuel booster:** rocket engine used as the principal force that allows a rocket or a missile to take off.

JIM HASKINS

Jim Haskins was born in 1941 in Montgomery, Alabama. After attending college in Arizona, Haskins went to New York City for graduate study and stayed.

Haskins's first book, *Diary of a Harlem Schoolteacher*, developed from his experience teaching Special Education at a New York City public school. After that, he wanted to write for young people: "I knew exactly the kinds of books I wanted to do—books about current events and books about important black people." He has written the biographies of many public figures, including Barbara Jordan. Haskins says, "I want children today, black and white, to be able to find books about black people and black history in case they want to read them."

WHAT I WANT TO BE WHEN I GROW UP

MARTHA BROOKS

Bus Windows Richard Estes, 1968-73, acrylic and oil on masonite, 48″ x 36″, Private collection

On the third Thursday afternoon of every month, I take my mother's hastily written note to the office where the school secretary, Mrs. Audrey Plumas, a nervous lady with red blotchy skin, looks at it and tells me I can go. Then I leave George J. Sherwood Junior High, walk down to the corner, and wait for the 2:47 bus which will get me downtown just in time for my four o'clock orthodontic[1] appointment.

I hate taking the bus. It's always too hot even in thirty-below-zero weather. The fumes and the lurching make me sick. The people are weird.

Mom says with the amount of money she's forking out to give me a perfect smile I shouldn't complain. "Andrew," she says cheerfully, "taking the bus is an education. It's a rare opportunity for people of all types and from all walks of life to be in an enforced environment that allows them to really get a close look at one another." She then adds, meaningfully, "Think of it as research for your life's work." She goes on like that even though she can't possibly know what she's talking about because she's a business executive who drives a brand-new air-conditioned Volvo to work every day.

I made the mistake, a while ago, of telling her I want to be a journalist when I grow up. Out of all the things I've ever wanted to be—an undersea photographer, a vet for the London Zoo, a missionary in Guatemala—she feels this latest choice is the most practical and has latched on to it like it's the last boat leaving the harbor.

---

1. **orthodontic** [ôr′ thə don′ tik]: having to do with straightening teeth.

She feels that, at fourteen, I have to start making "important career choices." This, in spite of the fact that my teeth stick out from having stopped sucking my thumb only six years ago.

On the bus last month, I happened to sit across the aisle from a girl with pasty white skin and pale eyes lined in some kind of indigo[2] gunk. We were right at the front, near the driver. The bus was so full there was no escape. She kept smiling like she had an imaginary friend. Every so often she'd lean forward and go, "Phe-ew," breathing right on me. The woman beside me wanted the whole bench to herself and edged me over with her enormous thighs until I was flattened against the metal railing. (I can't stand older women who wear stockings rolled, like floppy little doughnuts, down to their ankles.) She then took the shopping bag from her lap and mashed it between her ankles and mine as a further precaution[3] that I wouldn't take up any more room than I had coming to me. Hot, numb with misery, and totally grossed out, I closed my eyes and lost track of time. I went six extra stops and was fifteen minutes late for my appointment.

The old lady who runs the orthodontist's office also seems to run Dr. Fineman, who only appears, mole-like, to run his fingers along your gums and then scurries off to other patients in other rooms. This old lady doesn't like kids unless they are with a parent. The first few months I went with my mother. Mrs. G. Blahuta, Receptionist (that's the sign on this dinosaur's desk), smiled and told me what a brave boy I was. She even exchanged recipes with my mother. That was four years ago. This past time, when I arrived late and gasping because I'm slightly asthmatic,[4] Mrs. Blahuta (the orthodontist calls her Gladys; she has purple hair) scowled and asked me to come to the desk, where I stood, wishing I could die, while she shrilled at me about inconsiderate teenagers who think of no one but themselves and show so little responsibility and motivation it's a wonder they can dress themselves in the morning.

Shaking with humiliation, I sat down to wait my turn beside a blond girl with gold hairs on her beautiful tanned legs. She had been pretending to read a glamour magazine. Her eyebrows shot up as I sat down. She primly[5] inched away and gave me her

2. **indigo** [in′ də gō]: deep violet-blue.
3. **precaution** [pri kô′ shən]: something done beforehand in the hope of getting good results.
4. **asthmatic** [az mat′ ik]: having asthma, a disease that causes breathing difficulties.

back like she was a cat and I was some kind of bug she couldn't even be bothered to tease.

On the trip home another gorgeous pristine-type girl swayed onto the bus two stops after mine. She sat down in the empty seat in front of me and opened the window I'd been too weak from my previous ordeals to tackle. This lifesaving breeze hit my face, along with the sweet, stirring scent of her musky perfume. Gratefully I watched the back of her neck. (She wore her hair up. The backs of girls' necks make me crazy.)

After about five more stops a sandy-haired man, whose stomach rolled like a pumpkin over the belt of his green work pants, got on the bus and sat down beside this breath-stopping girl. She didn't even seem to know he was there, and with great interest stretched her long neck to get a close look at a passing trailer truck loaded with pigs. Their moist snouts poked at whatever air they could get at and you could tell they were on their way to the slaughterhouse. (Why else would pigs be spending a day in the city?)

The sandy-haired man readjusted his cap that was almost too small for his very large head. "Look at all them sausages!" he exclaimed, laughing really loudly at his dumb joke. The girl kept right on looking at the pigs. I could have died for her, but except for her nostrils that flared delicately and her slightly stiffened neck and shoulders, she didn't appear to be bothered at all.

The man playfully nudged her. "Hey!" he chortled, in a voice that could be heard all over the bus. "You like pork chops?"

She turned from the pigs (I noticed her incredibly long eyelashes that were light at the tips) and stared straight at him. His face went into a silly fixed smile. "Excuse me," she said cooly, and got up to leave.

"Oh, your stop comin' up, little lady?" he bellowed as he got up quickly. Pulling at his cap brim, he let her past.

She walked about four steps down the aisle and moved in beside an expensively dressed Chinese lady with bifocals[6] who looked suspiciously back at us, then frowned. I frowned at the fat man so she'd know it had been him, and not me, causing all the commotion.

I couldn't believe it when the man, calling more attention to himself,

5. **primly** [prim´ lē]: extremely neatly.
6. **bifocals** [bī fō´ kəlz]: lenses on glasses that have two sections, one for distant vision and the other for near vision.

The Bus Driver George Segal, 1962, plaster, wood, and metal, 7'5" x 51⅝" x 6'4¾", The Museum of Modern Art, New York

leaned forward and poked a business-type suit person! He said, in what possibly for him was a whisper, "Guess she don't like pigs." The suit person gave him a pained over-the-shoulder smile.

The man finally settled back. "I used to live on a farm. Yup. I did. I really did," he continued to nobody in particular because everybody near was pretending to look out of windows, or read, or be very concerned with what time their watches gave.

"Whew! It's hot!" He all of a sudden got up and reached over the suit person, ruffling his hair. "Oh sorry," he said. "Mind if I open this?" He tugged open the suit's window. The suit shot him a look that suggested he wasn't dealing with a full deck. Which he probably wasn't.

I prayed he would leave, but ten minutes later the girl of my dreams got off the bus. I was left staring at the pork chop man's thick, freckled neck.

His stop wasn't until one before mine. As we pulled away I watched him walk over and strike up a conversation with another complete stranger who was too polite to ignore him.

Like I said, you have to put up with some very weird people when you take the bus.

Today, I pleaded with my mother to drive me downtown. She lay on the couch popping painkillers because yesterday she fell and twisted an ankle and suffered a very small fracture as well. She isn't in a cast or anything and it's her left foot so she doesn't need it to drive with. When I asked her nicely for the second time, explaining that she wouldn't even have to get out of the car, she glared at me a moment and burst into tears. I don't understand why she's so selfish. I hope she gets a migraine[7] from watching soap operas all day.

Can you believe it? I was late

7. **migraine** [mī′grān]: a severe headache.

again for my appointment. I tried to explain to the purple-haired dinosaur that I'd missed my bus on account of being kept late in science class. (I had to rewrite a test I'd messed up the first time because I was away sick the day the teacher told us to study for it and my friend Gordon, the jerk, was supposed to tell me and forgot to.)

Mrs. Blahuta said snidely that she was surprised I was only twenty minutes late and did I intend to put in an appearance at my next monthly appointment or would they all be kept in suspense until the final moment of the working day, which was five o'clock. Sharp!

She kept me until every last person, except myself, had been checked over. At five to five she ushered me in to the orthodontist as his last appointment for the day. He processed me as if I were some dog in a laboratory and then Gladys dismissed me by holding out my next month's appointment slip like it was a bone I'd probably bury.

I got out onto the street, saw my bus departing, and made a silent vow that for at least a month I wasn't going to speak to any person over the age of eighteen.

At five twenty-two I boarded my bus and all the seats were taken. As we got under way, I suddenly felt sick. I clung to the nearest pole while the bus lurched, braked, accelerated, and picked up three or four passengers at every stop. Heated bodies armed with parcels, babies, books, and briefcases pressed past me. Into his microphone, the driver ordered everyone to the back. I didn't budge. When his voice began to sound as if it were coming from inside a vacuum cleaner, another wave of nausea overcame me and my hands, hot and wet, slipped down the pole.

I hate getting motion sickness. I'm sometimes so sensitive that just looking at, say, a movie of people going fast in a roller coaster can almost make me lose my last meal. Whenever I'm sick in the car, Mom says, "Fix your eyes on objects that are the furthest away. Don't look at anything that'll pass you by."

Remembering that, I turned to face the front of the bus. The furthest thing in my view was the pork chop man. As he was coming straight toward me, I shifted my gaze past his shoulder to a spot of blue that was, I guess, the sky. The bus took another shift and the sudden lurch swung me quickly around to where I'd been. I very nearly lost my battle with nausea to the skirts of a person wearing purple paisley.

Somebody gripped my arm, and said, "One of youse has to get up. This boy's going to be sick."

Immediately two people vacated their seats. Next thing I knew I was sitting beside a window with the pork chop man. He reached around behind me and tugged until wind hit my face.

"Hang your head out, now," he roared. "If you have to puke your guts out just go ahead and don't be shy." He patted my back in a fatherly way with one enormous hand while the other hung like a grizzly paw along the back end of my seat.

I did as I was told, breathed deeply for several seconds, and brought my head back in to have a look at him. I don't think I've ever seen such an enormous man. Up close, I realized he wasn't really so much fat as there was just an awful lot of him. "Name's Earl," he said, solemnly.

"Thanks, Earl," I said. "I'm Andrew."

"Don't have to thank me, Andrew. I joined A.A. two years ago. Haven't touched a drop since. I remember how it felt to be real sick."

I wanted to explain that I wasn't a drinker, but was overcome by another terrible feeling that I might lose control. Earl said, "Hold on, kid," and shoved my head out the window again.

We didn't talk much after that. It wasn't until my stop was coming up that I realized he'd just missed his.

I pulled the buzzer cord and said, "You missed your stop."

"How'd you know that?"

"I noticed you when you were on the bus one other time," I mumbled, embarrassed.

Earl sat back and looked straight ahead. He looked like a man who'd been struck by a thought that was almost too big to handle.

The bus arrived at my stop and Earl hurriedly got to his feet to let me past. I stepped off the bus with him right behind. On the street he said, still amazed, "You noticed me?"

The bus fumed noisily on past us.

"Yeah. Well—there was this girl, first. You came and sat beside her . . ." I trailed off.

"You know," said Earl, "just between you and me, city people aren't friendly. They don't notice nothing. See that old lady, there?"

At the light, an old girl tottered off the curb and started to cross the street. She carried two plastic Safeway bags full of groceries.

Out of the corner of his mouth, in a lisping whisper, Earl informed me, "If she was to fall and hurt herself just enough so she could still walk, not one person would stop and offer to help her home with those bags."

"That's true," I said, thinking that

if they did, they'd probably turn around and help themselves to her purse.

We started across the street. I felt better, now that we were off the bus. I actually started to feel a little hungry. I wondered how I was going to say good-bye to Earl. I was afraid he might want to talk to me for a long time. He walked slowly and I felt obliged to keep pace with him.

We reached the other side and stopped on the sidewalk. All the while he kept going on about the time he'd taken some guy to emergency at the General Hospital. The guy had almost bled to death before they could get anybody's attention.

Without hardly pausing to breathe, Earl cornered me with his desperately lonely eyes and launched into another story. I made out like I was really interested but to tell the truth I was thinking about my favorite TV program, which would be on that very moment, and about how Mom sits with me on the sofa, sometimes, while we eat our dinner and watch it together.

"Well," said Earl, too heartily, "I can see that you're going to be okay and I shouldn't keep you. Probably missed your supper, eh?"

He stuck out his hand, that massive freckled paw. Surprised, I took it and it surrounded mine in an amazingly gentle way. "Thanks," I said again.

"Told you not to mention it," said Earl. "We've all got to help each other out, don't we, buddy? But I can see I don't have to tell you that. You're different. You notice things."

MARTHA BROOKS

Martha Brooks was born in Manitoba, Canada. She grew up on the grounds of a tuberculosis sanatorium where her parents worked. When her sister left for college, Brooks says that her departure "drastically reduced the teenage population of the place where we lived." The remaining small society of very ill and very interesting people inspired some of the characters Brooks later created.

Brooks's teenage daughter was another source of inspiration. Brooks's books for young adults include *Paradise Café and Other Stories* and *Only a Paper Moon*.

MAURICE KENNY

I wrote in my journal
I had eaten only an orange
and some cheese this morning,
and drunk a pot of coffee dry.
When in truth, at dawn, I had eaten   5
lizards, coyotes, silver and cactus,
and a lone laborer in the desert.
I drank sky, sun and clouds;
my eyes consumed plains, mountains,
countries, continents;   10
worlds rumbled in my belly.
Tonight I slice and fork the western moon,
crunch on stars,
and drink the whine of wolves.

MAURICE KENNY

Maurice Kenny lives in Saranac Lake, New York, in the Iroquois country where he grew up. He has also spent a lot of time in Brooklyn, New York. "I hibernate in the city," he has said. But what Kenny has called his "home itch" always draws him back to the land where he feels he belongs.

Kenny's works include *Tokonwatonti* and *Greyhounding This America.*

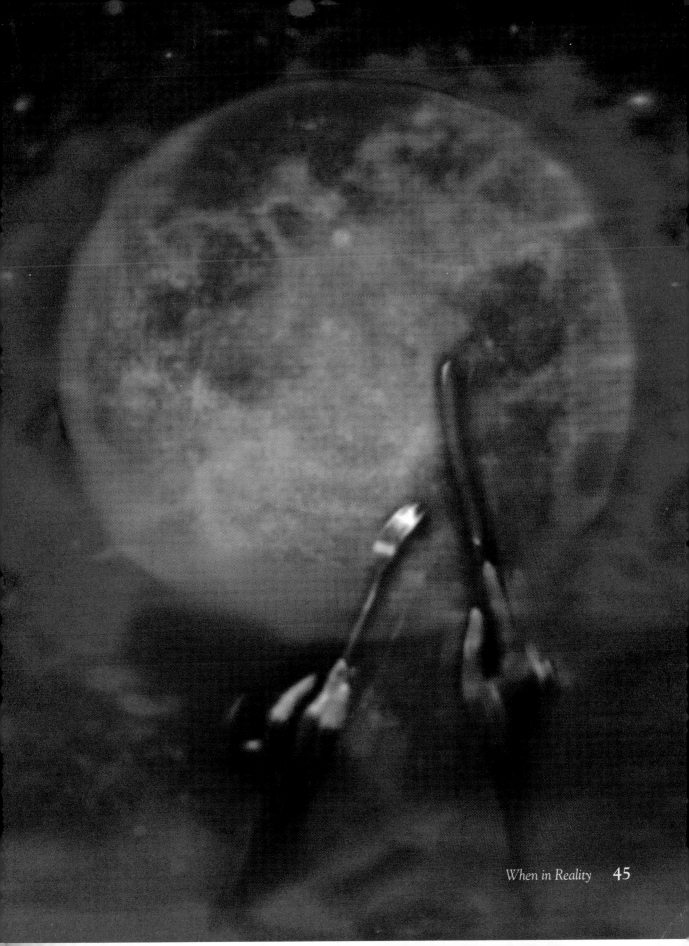

from The

True Confessions of Charlotte Doyle

AVI

For a second time I stood in the forecastle. The room was as dark and mean as when I'd first seen it. Now, however, I stood as a petitioner[1] in sailor's garb. A glum Fisk was at my side. It hadn't been easy to convince him I was in earnest about becoming one of the crew. Even when he begrudged[2] a willingness to believe in my sincerity he warned that agreement from the rest of the men would be improbable. He insisted I lay the matter before them immediately.

So it was that three men from Mr. Hollybrass's watch, Grimes, Dillingham, and Foley, were the next to hear my plea. As Fisk had foretold, they were contemplating[3] me and my proposal with very little evidence of favor.

1. **petitioner** [pə tish′ ən ər]: someone who asks a person in authority for a benefit.
2. **begrudged** [bi grudjd′]: was reluctant to admit.
3. **contemplating** [kon′ təm plāt ing]: looking at for a long time.

"I do mean it," I said, finding boldness with repetition, "I want to be the replacement for Mr. Johnson."

"You're a girl," Dillingham spat out contemptuously.[4]

"A *pretty* girl," Foley put in. It was not meant as a compliment. "Takes more than canvas britches to hide that."

"And a gentlewoman," was Grimes's addition, as though that was the final evidence of my essential uselessness.

"I want to show that I stand with you," I pleaded. "That I made a mistake."

"A mistake?" Foley snapped. "Two able-bodied men have died!"

"Besides," Dillingham agreed, "you'll bring more trouble than good."

"You can teach me," I offered.

"God's fist," Grimes cried. "She thinks this a school!"

"And the captain," Foley asked. "What'll he say?"

"He wants nothing to do with me," I replied.

"That's what he *says*. But you were his darling girl, Miss Doyle. We takes you in and he'll want you back again. Where will that put us?"

So it went, round and round. While the men made objections, while I struggled to answer them, Fisk said nothing.

Though I tried to keep my head up, my eyes steady, it was not easy. They looked at me as if I were some loathsome *thing*. At the same time, the more objections they made, the more determined I was to prove myself.

"See here, Miss Doyle," Dillingham concluded, "it's no simple matter. Understand, you sign on to the articles, so to speak, and you *are* on. No bolting to safe harbors at the first blow or when an ill word is flung your way. You're a hand or you're not a hand, and it won't go easy, that's all that can ever be promised."

"I know," I said.

"Hold out *your* hands," he demanded.

Fisk nudged me. I held them out, palms up.

4. **contemptuously** [kən temp′ chü əs lē]: scornfully, with disrespect.

Foley peered over them. "Like bloody cream," he said with disgust. "Touch mine!" he insisted and extended his. Gingerly, I touched one of them. His skin was like rough leather.

"That's the hands you'd get, miss. Like an animal. Is that what you want?"

"I don't care," I said stoutly.[5]

Finally it was Dillingham who said, "And are you willing to take your place in the rigging[6] too? Fair weather or foul?"

That made me pause.

Fisk caught the hesitation. "Answer," he prompted.

"Yes," I said boldly.

They exchanged glances. Then Foley asked, "What do the others think?"

Fisk shook his head and sighed. "No doubt they'll speak the same."

Suddenly Grimes said, "Here's what I say: let her climb to the royal yard.[7] If she does it and comes down whole, and *still* is willing to serve, then I say let her sign and be bloody damned like the rest of us."

"And do whatever she's called on to do!"

"No less!"

With no more than grunts the men seemed to agree among themselves. They turned toward me.

"*Now* what does Miss Doyle say?" Grimes demanded.

I swallowed hard, but all the same I gave yet another "Yes."

Foley came to his feet. "All right then. I'll go caucus[8] the others." Out he went.

Fisk and I retreated to the galley[9] while I waited for word. During that time he questioned me regarding my determination.

"Miss Doyle," he pressed, "you have agreed to climb to the top

5. **stoutly:** bravely.
6. **rigging:** the masts, sails, and ropes on a ship.
7. **royal yard:** the highest beam fastened across the mast, used to support the sail.
8. **caucus** [kô′ kəs]: consult, ask.
9. **galley** [gal′ ē]: kitchen of a ship.

of the royal yard. Do you know that's the highest sail on the main mast? One hundred and thirty feet up. You can reach it only two ways. You can shimmy up the mast itself. Or you can climb the shrouds,[10] using the ratlines[11] for your ladder."

I nodded as if I fully grasped what he was saying. The truth was I didn't even wish to listen. I just wanted to get past the test.

"And Miss Doyle," he went on, "if you slip and fall you'll be lucky to drop into the sea and drown quickly. No mortal could pluck you out fast enough to save you. Do you understand that?"

I swallowed hard but nodded. "Yes."

"Because if you're *not* lucky you'll crash to the deck. Fall that way and you'll either maim or kill yourself by breaking your neck. Still certain?"

"Yes," I repeated, though somewhat more softly.

"I'll give you this," he said with a look that seemed a mix of admiration and contempt, "Zachariah[12] was right. You're as steady a girl as ever I've met."

Foley soon returned. "We're agreed," he announced. "Not a one stands in favor of your signing on, Miss Doyle. Not with what you are. We're all agreed to that. But if you climb as high as the royal yard and make it down whole, and if you still want to sign on, you can come as equal. You'll get no more from us, Miss Doyle, but no less either."

Fisk looked at me for my answer.

"I understand," I said.

"All right then," Foley said. "The captain's still in his cabin and not likely to come out till five bells.[13] You can do it now."

"*Now?*" I quailed.[14]

"Now before never."

---

10. **shrouds:** pairs of ropes that reach from a mast to the side of a ship.
11. **ratlines:** small ropes that cross the shrouds of a ship, used as steps for climbing.
12. **Zachariah** [zak ə rī′ ə]
13. **five bells:** 2:30, 6:30, or 10:30; on ships, a certain number of bells are sounded each half hour to give the time.
14. **quailed** [kwāld]: shrank back in fear.

So it was that the four men escorted me onto the deck. There I found that the rest of the crew had already gathered.

Having fully committed myself, I was overwhelmed by my audacity.[15] The masts had always seemed tall, of course, but never so tall as they did at that moment. When I reached the deck and looked up my courage all but crumbled. My stomach turned. My legs grew weak.

Not that it mattered. Fisk escorted me to the mast as though I were being led to die at the stake. He seemed as grim as I.

15. **audacity** [ô das′ ə tē]: reckless daring, boldness.

To grasp fully what I'd undertaken to do, know again that the height of the mainmast towered one hundred and thirty feet from the deck. This mast was, in fact, three great rounded lengths of wood, trees, in truth, affixed one to the end of the other. Further, it supported four levels of sails, each of which bore a different name. In order, bottom to top, these were called the main yard, topsail, topgallant, and finally royal yard.

My task was to climb to the top of the royal yard. And come down. In one piece. If I succeeded I'd gain the opportunity of making the climb fifty times a day.

As if reading my terrified thoughts Fisk inquired gravely, "How will you go, Miss Doyle? Up the mast or on the ratlines?"

Once again I looked up. I could not possibly climb the mast directly. The stays and shrouds with their ratlines would serve me better.

"Ratlines," I replied softly.

"Then up you go."

I will confess it, at that moment my nerves failed. I found myself unable to move. With thudding heart I looked frantically around. The members of the crew, arranged in a crescent, were standing like death's own jury.

It was Barlow who called out, "A blessing goes with you, Miss Doyle."

To which Ewing added, "And this advice, Miss Doyle. Keep your eyes steady on the ropes. Don't you look down. Or up."

For the first time I sensed that some of them at least wanted me to succeed. The realization gave me courage.

With halting steps and shallow breath, I approached the rail only to pause when I reached it. I could hear a small inner voice crying, "Don't! Don't!"

But it was also then that I heard Dillingham snicker, "She'll not have the stomach."

I reached up, grasped the lowest deadeye,[16] and hauled myself atop the rail. That much I had done before. Now, I maneuvered to

16. **deadeye** [ded′ ī]: round, flat, wooden block that fastens the shrouds of a ship.

the outside so that I would be leaning *into* the rigging and could even rest on it.

Once again I looked at the crew, *down* at them, I should say. They were staring up with blank expressions.

Recollecting Ewing's advice, I shifted my eyes and focused them on the ropes before me. Then, reaching as high as I could into one of the middle shrouds, and grabbing a ratline, I began to climb.

The ratlines were set about sixteen inches one above the other, so that the steps I had to take were wide for me. I needed to pull as much with arms as climb with legs. But line by line I did go up, as if ascending an enormous ladder.

After I had risen some seventeen feet I realized I'd made a great mistake. The rigging stood in sets, each going to a different level of the mast. I could have taken one that stretched directly to the top. Instead, I had chosen a line which went only to the first trestletree, to the top of the lower mast.

For a moment I considered backing down and starting afresh. I stole a quick glance below. The crew's faces were turned up toward me. I understood that they would take the smallest movement down as retreat. I had to continue.

And so I did.

Now I was climbing inside the lank gray-white sails, ascending, as it were, into a bank of dead clouds.

Beyond the sails lay the sea, slate-gray and ever rolling. Though the water looked calm, I could feel the slow pitch and roll it caused in the ship. I realized suddenly how much harder this climb would be if the wind were blowing and we were well underway. The mere thought made the palms of my hands grow damp.

Up I continued till I reached the main yard. Here I snatched another glance at the sea, and was startled to see how much bigger it had grown. Indeed, the more I saw of it the *more* there was. In contrast, the *Seahawk* struck me as having suddenly grown smaller. The more I saw of *her*, the *less* she was!

I glanced aloft. To climb higher I now had to edge myself out upon the trestletree and then once again move up the next set of ratlines as I'd done before. But at twice the height!

Wrapping one arm around the mast—even up here it was too big to reach around completely—I grasped one of the stays and edged out. At the same moment the ship dipped, the world seemed to twist and tilt down. My stomach lurched. My heart pounded. My head swam. In spite of myself I closed my eyes. I all but slipped, saving myself only by a sudden grasp of a line before the ship yawed the opposite way. I felt sicker yet. With everwaning strength I clung on for dearest life. Now the full folly of what I was attempting burst upon me with grotesque reality. It had been not only stupid, but suicidal. I would never come down alive!

And yet I had to climb. This was my restitution.[17]

When the ship was steady again, I grasped the furthest rigging, first with one hand, then the other, and dragged myself higher. I was heading for the topsail, fifteen feet further up.

Pressing myself as close as possible into the rigging, I continued to strain upward, squeezing the ropes so tightly my hands cramped. I even tried curling my toes about the ratlines.

At last I reached the topsail spar,[18] but discovered it was impossible to rest there. The only place to pause was three *times* higher than the distance I'd just come, at the trestletree just below the topgallant spar.

By now every muscle in my body ached. My head felt light, my heart an anvil. My hands were on fire, the soles of my feet raw. Time and again I was forced to halt, pressing my face against the rigging with eyes closed. Then, in spite of what I'd been warned not to do, I opened them and peered down. The *Seahawk* was like a wooden toy. The sea looked greater still.

I made myself glance up. Oh, so far to go! How I forced myself to move I am not sure. But the thought of backing down now was just as frightening. Knowing only that I could not stay still, I crept upward, ratline by ratline, taking what seemed to be forever with

17. **restitution** [res′ tə tü′ shən]: act of making up for damage or injury done.
18. **topsail spar** [top′ sāl′ spär]: strong pole used to support the sail that is above the lowest sail on a mast.

each rise until I finally reached the level just below the topgallant spar.

A seasoned sailor would have needed two minutes to reach this point. I had needed thirty!

Though I felt the constant roll of the ship, I had to rest there. What seemed like little movement on deck became, up high, wild swings and turns through treacherous air.

I gagged, forced my stomach down, drew breath, and looked out. Though I didn't think it possible, the ocean appeared to have grown greater yet. And when I looked down, the upturned faces of the crew appeared like so many tiny bugs.

There were twenty-five or so more feet to climb. Once again I grasped the rigging and hauled myself up.

This final climb was torture. With every upward pull the swaying of the ship seemed to increase. Even when not moving myself, I was flying through the air in wild, wide gyrations. The horizon kept shifting, tilting, dropping. I was increasingly dizzy, nauseous, terrified, certain that with every next moment I would slip and fall to death. I paused again and again, my eyes on the rigging inches from my face, gasping and praying as I had never prayed before. My one hope was that, nearer to heaven now, I could make my desperation heard!

Inch by inch I continued up. Half an inch! Quarter inches! But then at last with trembling fingers, I touched the spar of the royal yard. I had reached the top.

Once there I endeavored to rest again. But there the metronome[19] motion of the mast was at its most extreme, the *Seahawk* turning, tossing, swaying as if trying to shake me off—like a dog throwing droplets of water from its back. And when I looked beyond I saw a sea that was infinity itself, ready, eager to swallow me whole.

I had to get back down.

As hard as it was to climb up, it was, to my horror, harder returning. On the ascent I could see where I was going. Edging down I had to grope blindly with my feet. Sometimes I tried to look. But when I did the sight of the void below was so sickening, I was forced to close my eyes.

Each groping step downward was a nightmare. Most times my foot found only air. Then, as if to mock my terror, a small breeze at last sprang up. Sails began to fill and snap, puffing in and out, at times smothering me. The tossing of the ship grew—if that were possible—more extreme.

Down I crept, past the topgallant where I paused briefly on the trestletree, then down along the longest stretch, toward the mainyard. It was there I fell.

I was searching with my left foot for the next ratline. When I found a hold and started to put my weight upon it, my foot, slipping on the slick tar surface, shot forward. The suddenness of it made me lose my grip. I tumbled backward, but in such a way that my legs became entangled in the lines. There I hung, *head downward.*

I screamed, tried to grab something. But I couldn't. I clutched madly at nothing, till my hand brushed against a dangling rope. I grabbed for it, missed, and grabbed again. Using all my strength, I levered myself up and, wrapping my arms into the lines, made a veritable[20] knot of myself, mast, and rigging. Oh, how I wept! my entire body shaking and trembling as though it would break apart.

19. **metronome** [met′ rə nōm]: device that moves back and forth in musical time for practicing on musical instruments; here, the back and forth motion of the mast.

20. **veritable** [ver′ ə tə bəl]: real, actual.

When my breathing became somewhat normal, I managed to untangle first one arm, then my legs. I was free.

I continued down. By the time I reached the mainyard I was numb and whimpering again, tears coursing from my eyes.

I moved to the shrouds I'd climbed, and edged myself past the lowest of the sails.

As I emerged from under it, the crew gave out a great "Huzzah!"

Oh, how my heart swelled with exaltation!

Finally, when I'd reached close to the very end, Barlow stepped forward, beaming, his arms uplifted. "Jump!" he called. "Jump!"

But now, determined to do it all myself, I shook my head. Indeed, in the end I dropped down on my own two India-rubber legs—and tumbled to the deck.

No sooner did I land than the crew gave me another "Huzzah!" With joyous heart I staggered to my feet. Only then did I see Captain Jaggery push through the knot of men and come to stand before me.

A V I

Avi Wortis was born in 1937 in New York City. He grew up in a family of readers, writers, and story-tellers. "I do believe that if you want to be a writer you have to read a lot," he says.

Avi first wrote plays and novels for adults. When he became a father, he began inventing stories just for children and young people—such as the adventure story called "Night Journeys"—that you might not be able to put down.

The Kitchen Knight

MARGARET HODGES

In the springtime, when the Round Table was in its glory, King Arthur always held a high feast. But before he sat down at the table, he liked to hear something new, or some adventure. Once, when he was waiting to keep the feast at a seaside castle, he looked from a window and saw in the courtyard a tall young man riding a poor horse and followed by a dwarf. The young man dismounted and the dwarf led the horse away.

Then the stranger came into the hall. He was a goodly young fellow. His manner was friendly, modest, and mild. He was big, broad in the shoulders, and handsome, the very sort to bring news of an adventure. So Arthur made him welcome to the feast and sat down at the table with all his knights around him.

"God bless you, King Arthur," said the young stranger, "and God bless the fellowship of the Table Round. I have come to ask you for three favors. Today I ask for the first. Give me meat and drink for one year. At the end of the year I will ask my other two favors."

"Granted," said Arthur, "for my heart tells me that you will prove to be a man of great worth. What is your name?"

"I cannot tell you," said the youth.

"A goodly young man like you does not know his own name?" said the king in jest. Then he told Sir Kay, his steward,[1] to give the youth the best of meat and drink and all other things that a lord's son should have.

"There is no need for that expense," Kay said to himself. "A gentleman would have asked for a good horse and armor. This fellow is a peasant, as overgrown as a weed, and wanting nothing but meat and drink. He can work and eat in the kitchen. At the end of a year he will be fat as a hog."

Now Arthur's best knight, Sir Lancelot, was kind to the young man because of his own great gentleness and courtesy, while Sir Kay was always rude to the stranger. But the boy took his place in the kitchen and shared the work without complaint. When the kitchen lads competed in sports, the unknown youth was a winner. When the knights jousted,[2] he was always watching.

Single Knight on Horseback
Illuminated manuscript page, from Codex Manesse, 14th Century, University Library, Heidelberg, Germany

1. **steward** [stü′ ərd]: man who has charge of food and table service.
2. **jousted** [joust′ əd]: fought on horseback, armed with spears called lances.

So a year passed, and once again the king wished to hear of some adventure before he sat down at the springtime feast. Then there came a squire[3] who said to the king, "Sir, you may sit down to eat, for here comes a lady with a strange adventure to tell."

At once, a proud lady came into the hall and said, "Sir, I have come to you because your knights are the noblest in the world. I ask one of them to help my sister, who is held prisoner in her castle."

"What is her name?" asked the king. "And where does she dwell?"

"I will not tell you," said the lady. "But the tyrant[4] who holds her prisoner in her castle is Sir Ironside, the Red Knight of the Red Plain. He is evil, and as strong as seven men."

Then the tall kitchen boy stepped forward and knelt before the king. "Sir," he said, "I have been for twelve months in your kitchen and have had my meat and drink as you promised. Now I will ask my last favors. Let me have this adventure, and let Sir Lancelot ride after me. If I win my spurs,[5] let him make me a knight."

The king was well pleased. "All this shall be done," he said.

But the lady cried, "For shame! Must I have a kitchen boy for my champion?" And she took her horse and rode off.

Then there came into the courtyard the same dwarf who had arrived with the stranger a year before. He was leading a fine horse which carried on its back a breastplate and sword. The kitchen boy took the sword and armor, and mounted the horse. Then he asked Sir Lancelot to follow, and without shield or lance rode after the lady. The dwarf rode behind.

Sir Kay rode after them and ordered them to stop, for he thought the kitchen boy unworthy to be the champion of so proud a lady. The boy rode on.

Sir Kay called angrily, "Fellow, do you not know my voice?"

The boy turned his horse and answered, "I know you for the most ill-mannered knight of King Arthur's court."

3. **squire** [skwīr]: young nobleman who served a knight until he himself became a knight.
4. **tyrant** [tī′rənt]: cruel or unjust ruler.
5. **win my spurs** [spěrz]: idiom meaning "succeed."

Kay put his spear in the saddle rest and rode straight upon him, and the kitchen boy came fast upon Kay with his sword in hand. He thrust Kay's spear aside and struck such a blow that Kay fell from his horse and lay stunned on the ground. Then the kitchen boy took Sir Kay's spear and shield. He put the dwarf on Kay's horse, mounted his own, and rode after the lady.

Sir Lancelot had seen the whole adventure. When he and his squires caught up with the youth, he said, "You fought well, more like a giant than a man."

"Sir, do you think I shall some day be worthy of knighthood?" asked the kitchen boy.

"You are worthy this day," said Lancelot. "I will knight you here and now. But first, tell me your name and family."

"I am Gareth of Orkney, from the islands far to the north, and I am nephew to the king," said the young man, "but the king must not know until I have truly won my spurs."

Then Lancelot dubbed Gareth a knight and returned to Arthur's court, while his squires had to carry Sir Kay on a shield.

Sir Gareth rode on and overtook the proud lady. "Is it you again?" she said. "You smell of the kitchen and your clothes are foul with kitchen grease under your armor. Do you think I like you better for wounding that knight? You did not fight fairly. Go away, you lubber,[6] you turner of spits[7] and washer of ladles."

"Madam," said Gareth, "say what you will, I shall fight against any knight who bars your way. I will follow this adventure to the end, or die in the attempt."

"You would not face the Red Knight of the Red Plain for all the soup in the kitchen," said she.

"I will try," he said.

At the day's end they came to a castle where a knight offered them good cheer and set a table for them. But the lady said, "This kitchen boy is more fit for pig-sticking than for sitting with a lady of high degree."

6. **lubber** [lub′ər]: big, clumsy, stupid fellow.
7. **spits:** sharp-pointed, slender bars on which meat is roasted.

The knight of the castle was ashamed of her words. He took Gareth to another table and ate there with him, leaving the proud lady to sit by herself.

The next day Gareth rode on with her, and she never gave him a civil word. Then they came to a black field and saw a black hawthorn[8] tree with a black banner and a black shield hanging on it. Beside the tree stood a great black horse covered with trappings of black silk. And on the horse sat a knight in black armor, barring the way.

"Lady," said he, "have you brought this knight to be your champion against me?"

"No," she said, "he is only a kitchen boy, and I would gladly be rid of him."

"Then I will take his horse and armor from him," said the knight in black armor. "It would be a shame to do more harm than that to a kitchen boy."

"I am about to cross your field," said Gareth. "Let us see if you can take my horse and armor." Then they rode against each other and came together with a sound like thunder. The knight in black armor smote Gareth with many strokes and hurt him full sore, but Gareth fought back and brought him to the ground. He won the black horse and the black armor, and rode after the lady.

"Away, kitchen boy," she said. "Out of the wind. The smell of your clothes offends me. Alas, that such a knave[9] as you should fell so good a knight, and all by luck. But the Red Knight will kill you. Away, flee while you can."

"Lady," said Gareth, "you are not courteous to speak to me as you do. Always you say that I should be beaten by knights that we meet, but for all that, they lie in the dust."

Then they came to a meadow, new mown and full of blue pavilions.[10] The lady said, "A noble knight comes in fair weather with five hundred

---

8. **hawthorn** [hô´ thôrn]: small tree of the rose family with fragrant white, red, or pink flowers.
9. **knave** [nāv]: tricky, dishonest man.
10. **pavilions** [pə vil´ yənz]: tent-like open buildings used for shelter.

knights to joust in this meadow. You had better flee before he sets upon you with all his knights."

"If he is noble, he will not set upon me with five hundred knights," said Gareth. "And if they come one at a time, I will face them as long as I live."

Then the lady was ashamed and said, "I pray you, save yourself while you can. You and your horse have fought hard and long, and you will have the hardest fight of all when we come to my sister's castle."

Gareth answered, "Be that as it may, I shall deal with this knight now, and we shall come to your sister's castle while it is still daylight."

"What manner of man are you!" said the lady. "Never did a woman treat a knight so shamefully as I have you, and you have always answered me courteously. Only a man of noble blood would do so."

Two Knights on Horseback Fighting Illuminated manuscript page, from Codex Manesse, 14th Century, University Library, Heidelberg, Germany

He answered, "I am Gareth, the king's nephew. I ate my meat in his kitchen so that I might know who are my true friends, and I never minded your words, for the more you angered me, the better I fought."

"Alas," she said, "forgive me."

"With all my heart," said Gareth. "And now that we are friends, I think there is no knight living but I am strong enough to face him."

Then the knight of the blue pavilions clad all in blue armor came against Gareth, and Gareth rode against him with such force that their spears broke in pieces and their horses fell to the earth. But the two knights sprang to their feet and drew their swords and gave many great strokes until their shields and their armor were hewn to bits. At last, Sir Gareth gave such a blow that the blue knight begged for mercy, saying, "I and my five hundred knights shall always be at your command."

Then he made Gareth and the lady welcome in his own pavilion and Sir Gareth told how he was going to fight against the Red Knight of the Red Plain to relieve the fair lady's sister.

The blue knight answered, "The Knight of the Red Plain is the most fearsome and perilous[11] knight now living." And he asked the lady, "Is it not your sister Linesse who is besieged[12] by the Red Knight? Is not your name Linette?"

"All this is true," she said.

Then Gareth and Linette rode on together until they came close to the Castle Perilous, and they saw that from the branch of a sycamore tree[13] nearby there hung a great ivory horn.

"Fair sir," said Linette, "if any knight blows this horn, the Red Knight will come to do battle. His strength increases until midday, so do not blow the horn before high noon."

"I will fight him at his strongest," said Sir Gareth, and he blew the horn so eagerly that the Castle Perilous rang with the sound, and those within looked over the walls and out the windows. Then the Red Knight armed himself, and all was blood-red—his armor, spear, and shield—and he rode to a little valley close by the castle so that all within and without might see the battle.

Linette pointed to a far window in a tower of the castle, and said, "Yonder is my sister Linesse."

Sir Gareth said, "Even from afar, she seems a fair lady. I will gladly do battle for her." Then he raised his hand to her and in her far window the lady raised her hand to him.

But the Red Knight called to Sir Gareth, "Look not at her but at me. She is my lady and I have fought many battles for her."

---

11. **perilous** [per´ ə ləs]: dangerous.
12. **besieged** [bi sējd´]: surrounded by armed forces in order to force surrender.
13. **sycamore tree** [sik´ ə môr]: tall shade tree with broad leaves.

"I think it was a waste of labor," said Gareth. "To love one who does not love you is great folly.[14] I will rescue her or die in the attempt."

"Talk no more with me," said the Red Knight. "Make yourself ready."

Then they put their spears in their rests and came together with all the might they had. They smote each other with such force that both knights fell to the ground, and all within the castle thought their necks had been broken. But they rose and put their shields before them and ran together like two fierce lions. They battled till it was past noon. Again and again they came face to face, locked in struggle, and now and again they unlaced their helmets and sat down to rest. And when Gareth's helmet was off, he looked at the distant window, and the faraway face of the lady Linesse made his heart light and joyful.

At last the Red Knight smote Gareth such a blow that Gareth lost his sword and fell to the ground.

Then Linette cried out, "Sir Gareth, what has become of your courage? My sister is watching you."

When Gareth heard that, he leaped to his feet and picked up his sword. He struck the sword from the Red Knight's hand and smote him on the helmet so that he fell, and Gareth pinned him to the earth. Then the Red Knight asked for mercy, and many of his noble knights came to Sir Gareth and begged him to spare the life of the Red Knight. "For," said they, "his death will not help you, and his misdeeds cannot be undone. Therefore let him right the wrongs he has done, and we will all be your men."

"Fair lords," said Gareth, "I will release him. But let him yield himself to the lady of the castle."

"This I will do," said the Red Knight, and he went to the castle to ask forgiveness of the lady Linesse. She received him kindly. But when Gareth went to the castle, she sent a message to the gateway, saying, "Go your way, Sir Knight, until I know more of you."

Then secretly she sent a knight to follow Gareth and to capture the dwarf so that she could question him.

14. **folly** [fol′ē]: foolishness.

Knight with Maiden Illuminated page, from Codex Manesse, 14th Century, University Library, Heidelberg , Germany

Sir Gareth rode away with his dwarf sorrowfully. They rode here and there, and knew not where they rode, until it was dark night. Then, weary and sick at heart for love of the faraway lady, he gave his horse into the care of the dwarf and lay down to rest with his head on his shield.

And while Gareth slept, the knight sent by the lady came softly behind the dwarf. He picked him up and rode away with him as fast as ever he might. But the dwarf cried out to Sir Gareth for help. And Sir Gareth awoke and followed them through marsh[15] and moor[16] until he lost sight of them. Many times his horse and he plunged over their heads in deep mire, for he did not know his way. And while Sir Gareth was in such danger, the dwarf was telling the lady Linesse that her unknown champion was Sir Gareth of Orkney, nephew of King Arthur.

When at last Gareth found the castle again, he was angry, and he drew his sword, shouting to the guards that they must give back his dwarf.

The lady Linesse said, "I would speak with Sir Gareth, but he must not know who I am." Then the drawbridge was let down and the gate was opened. And when Sir Gareth rode in, his dwarf came to take the horse.

15. **marsh:** soft, wet land.
16. **moor:** open, rolling land, usually covered with short grasses and other vegetation.

"Oh, little fellow," said Sir Gareth, "I have been in much danger for your sake."

He washed, and the dwarf brought him clothing fit for a knight to wear. And when Gareth went into the great hall, he saw the lady Linesse disguised as a strange princess. They exchanged many fair words and kind looks. And Gareth thought, "Would to God that the faraway lady of the tower might prove to be as fair as this lady!"

They danced together, and the lady Linesse said to herself, "Now I know that I would rather Sir Gareth were mine than any king or prince in this world, and if I may not have him as my husband, I will have none. He is my first love, and he shall be the last."

And she told him that she was the same lady he had done battle for, and the one who had caused his dwarf to be stolen away "to know certainly who you were."

Then into the dance came Linette, who had ridden with him along so many perilous paths, and Sir Gareth took the lady Linesse by one hand and Linette by the other, and he was more glad than ever before.

Thus ends the tale of Sir Gareth of Orkney.

MARGARET HODGES

Margaret Hodges was born in 1911 in Indianapolis, Indiana. She went east for college. Much later, when her children were grown, Hodges went back to school for a Master's degree in library science. She then began a long career as a children's librarian in Pittsburgh, Pennsylvania, and as a storyteller on radio. All along, she was writing.

Hodges has written numerous kinds of books. One kind she calls "stories based on the adventures and misadventures of my three sons." She has also written biographies of "little-known or disregarded characters who have contributed in an important way to history." One is *Hopkins of the Mayflower: Portrait of a Dissenter*.

For young people, Hodges has written travel books and has retold folktales, myths, and legends such as "The Kitchen Knight."

John Savage

The Getaway

Whenever I get sleepy at the wheel, I always stop for coffee. This time, I was going along in western Texas and I got sleepy. I saw a sign that said GAS EAT, so I pulled off. It was long after midnight: What I expected was a place like a bunch of others, where the coffee tastes like copper and the flies never sleep.

What I found was something else. The tables were painted wood, and they looked as if nobody ever spilled the ketchup. The counter was spick-and-span. Even the smell was OK, I swear it.

Nobody was there, as far as customers. There was just this one old boy—really only about forty, getting gray above the ears—behind the counter. I sat down at the counter and ordered coffee and apple pie. Right away he got me started feeling sad.

I have a habit: I divide people up. Winners and losers. This old boy behind the counter was the kind that they *mean* well; they can't do enough for you, but their eyes have this gentle, faraway look, and they can't win. You know? With their clean shirt and their little bow tie? It makes you feel sad just to look at them. Only take my tip: Don't feel too sad.

He brought the coffee steaming hot, and it tasted like coffee. "Care for cream and sugar?" he asked. I said, "Please," and the cream was fresh and cold and thick. The pie was good, too.

A car pulled up outside. The old boy glanced out to see if they wanted gas, but they didn't. They came right in. The tall one said, "Two coffees. Do you have a road map we could look at?"

"I think so," the old boy said. He got their coffee first, and then started rooting through a pile of papers by the telephone, looking for a map. It was easy to see he was the type nothing's too much trouble for. Tickled to be of service.

I'm the same type myself, if you want to know. I watched the old boy hunting for his map, and I felt like I was looking in a mirror.

After a minute or two, he came up with the map. "This one's a little out of date, but . . . " He put it on the counter, beside their coffee.

The two men spread out the map and leaned over it. They were well dressed, like a couple of feed merchants.[1] The tall one ran his finger along the Rio Grande[2] and shook his head. "I guess there's no place to get across, this side of El Paso."[3]

He said it to his pal, but the old boy behind the counter heard him and lit up like a light bulb. "You trying to find the best way south? I might be able to help you with that."

"How?"

"Just a minute." He spent a lot of time going through the papers by the telephone again. "Thought I might have a

---

1. **feed merchants:** those who sell food for farm animals.
2. **Rio Grande** [rē′ ō grand]: river that forms part of the boundary between the United States and Mexico.
3. **El Paso** [el pas′ ō]: city in western Texas, on the Rio Grande.

newer map," he said. "Anything recent would show the Hackett Bridge. Anyway, I can tell you how to find it."

"Here's a town called Hackett," the tall one said, still looking at the map. "It's on the river, just at the end of a road. Looks like a pretty small place."

"Not any more. It's just about doubled since they built the bridge."

"What happens on the other side?" The short one asked the question, but both of the feed-merchant types were paying close attention.

"Pretty fair road, clear to Chihuahua.[4] It joins up there with the highway out of El Paso and Juarez."[5]

The tall man finished his coffee, folded the map, put it in his pocket, and stood up. "We'll take your map with us," he said.

The old boy seemed startled, like a new kid at school when somebody pokes him in the nose to show him who's boss. However, he just shrugged and said, "Glad to let you have it."

The feed merchants had a little conference on the way out; talking in whispers. Then they stopped in the middle of the floor, turned around, reached inside their jackets, and pulled guns on us. Automatic pistols, I think they were. "You sit where you are and don't move," the tall one said to me. "And *you*, get against the wall."

Both of us did exactly what they wanted. I told you we were a lot alike.

The short man walked over and pushed one of the keys of the cash register. "Every little bit helps," he said, and he scooped the money out of the drawer. The tall man set the telephone on the floor, put his foot on it, and jerked the wires out. Then they ran to their car and got in. The short man leaned out the window and shot out one of my tires. Then they took off fast.

I looked at the old boy behind the counter. He seemed a little pale, but he didn't waste any time. He took a screwdriver out of a drawer and squatted down beside the telephone. I said, "It doesn't always pay to be nice to people."

4. **Chihuahua** [chē wä′ wä]: state in northern Mexico; its capital has the same name.

5. **Juarez** [hwär′ es]: city in northern Mexico, across the Rio Grande from El Paso, Texas.

He laughed and said, "Well, it doesn't usually cost anything," and went on taking the base plate off the telephone. He was a fast worker, actually. His tongue was sticking out of the corner of his mouth. In about five minutes he had a dial tone coming out of the receiver. He dialed a number and told the Rangers about the men and their car. "They did?" he said. "Well, well, well. . . . No, not El Paso. They took the Hackett turnoff." After he hung up, he said, "It turns out those guys robbed a supermarket in Wichita Falls."[6]

I shook my head. "They sure had me fooled. I thought they looked perfectly all right."

The old boy got me another cup of coffee, and opened himself a bottle of pop. "They fooled me, too, at first." He wiped his mouth. "Then I got a load of their shoulder holsters when they leaned on the counter to look at the map. Anyway, they had mean eyes, I thought. Didn't you?"

"Well, I didn't at the time."

We drank without talking for a while, getting our nerves back in shape. A pair of patrol cars went roaring by outside and squealed their tires around the Hackett turnoff.

I got to thinking, and I thought of the saddest thing yet. "You *knew* there was something wrong with those guys, but you still couldn't keep from helping them on their way."

He laughed. "Well, the world's a tough sort of place at best, is how I look at it."

"I can understand showing them the map," I said, "but I would never have told about the bridge. Now there's not even an outside chance of catching them. If you'd kept your mouth shut, there'd at least be some hope."

"There isn't any—"

"Not a shred," I went on. "Not with a car as fast as they've got."

The way the old boy smiled made me feel better about him and me. "I don't mean there isn't any hope," he said. "I mean there isn't any bridge."

6. **Wichita Falls** [wich′ i tô′]: city in northern Texas.

NOTHING TO BE AFRAID OF

JAN MARK

"Robin won't give you any trouble," said Auntie Lynn. "He's very quiet."

Anthea knew how quiet Robin was. At present he was sitting under the table, and until Auntie Lynn had mentioned his name, she had forgotten that he was there.

Auntie Lynn put an overnight bag on the armchair.

"There's plenty of clothes, so you won't need to do any washing, and there's a spare pair of pajamas in case—well, you know. In case . . ."

"Yes," said Mum firmly. "He'll be all right. I'll ring you tonight and let you know how he's getting along." She looked at the clock. "Now, hadn't *you* better be getting along?"

She saw Auntie Lynn to the front door and Anthea heard them saying good-bye to each other. Mum almost told Auntie Lynn to stop worrying and have a good time, which would have been a mistake because Auntie Lynn was going up north to a funeral.

Deep in the Forest Rex Lau, 1985, oil on carved hydro-stone, 26" x 24", Private collection

Auntie Lynn was not really an aunt, but she had once been at school with Anthea's mum, and she was the kind of person who couldn't manage without a handle to her name; so Robin was not Anthea's cousin. Robin was not anything much, except four years old, and he looked a lot younger; probably because nothing ever happened to him. Auntie Lynn kept no pets that might give Robin germs, and never bought him toys that had sharp corners to dent him or wheels that could be swallowed. He wore knitted balaclava[1] helmets and pompom hats in winter to protect his tender ears, and a knitted undershirt in summer in case he overheated himself and caught a chill from his own sweat.

"Perspiration," said Auntie Lynn.

His face was as pale and flat as a saucer of milk, and his eyes floated in it like drops of cod-liver oil.[2] This was not so surprising, as he was full to the back teeth with cod-liver oil; also with extract of malt, concentrated orange juice, and calves'-foot jelly. When you picked him up you expected him to squelch, like a hot-water bottle full of half-set custard.

Anthea lifted the tablecloth and looked at him.

"Hello, Robin."

Robin stared at her with his flat eyes and went back to sucking his wooly doggy that had flat eyes also, of sewn-on felt, because glass ones might find their way into Robin's appendix and cause damage. Anthea wondered how long it would be before he noticed that his mother had gone. Probably he wouldn't, any more than he would notice when she came back.

Mum closed the front door and joined Anthea in looking under the table at Robin. Robin's mouth turned down at the corners, and Anthea hoped he would cry so that they could cuddle him. It seemed impolite to cuddle him before he needed it. Anthea was afraid to go any closer.

1. **balaclava** [bä lə klä′ və]: close-fitting, knitted woolen cap that covers the head, neck, and tops of the shoulders.
2. **cod-liver oil** [kod′ liv′ ər]: oil from the liver of codfish, used in medicine as a source of vitamins A and D.

"What a little troll," said Mum sadly, lowering the tablecloth. "I suppose he'll come out when he's hungry."

Anthea doubted it.

Robin didn't want any lunch or any tea.

"Do you think he's pining?" said Mum. Anthea did not. Anthea had a nasty suspicion that he was like this all the time. He went to bed without making a fuss and fell asleep before the light was out, as if he were too bored to stay awake. Anthea left her bedroom door open, hoping that he would have a nightmare so that she could go in and comfort him, but Robin slept all night without a squeak, and woke in the morning as flat faced as before. Wall-eyed Doggy looked more excitable than Robin did.

"If only we had a proper garden," said Mum, as Robin went under the table again, leaving his breakfast eggs scattered round the plate. "He might run about."

Anthea thought that this was unlikely, and in any case they didn't have a proper garden, only a yard at the back and a stony strip in front, without a fence.

"Can I take him to the park?" said Anthea.

Mum looked doubtful. "Do you think he wants to go?"

"No," said Anthea, peering under the tablecloth. "I don't think he wants to do anything, but he can't sit there all day."

"I bet he can," said Mum. "Still, I don't think he should. All right, take him to the park, but keep quiet about it. I don't suppose Lynn thinks you're safe in traffic."

"He might tell her."

"Can he talk?"

Robin, still clutching wall-eyed Doggy, plodded beside her all the way to the park, without once trying to jam his head between the library railings or get run over by a bus.

"Hold my hand, Robin," Anthea said as they left the house, and he clung to her like a lamprey.[3]

3. **lamprey** [lam′ prē]: ocean and freshwater animal with a body like an eel's body and a large, round mouth for attaching itself to other fish.

The park was not really a park at all; it was a garden. It did not even pretend to be a park, and the notice by the gate said KING STREET GARDENS, in case anyone tried to use it as a park. The grass was as green and as flat as the front-room carpet, but the front-room carpet had a path worn across it from the door to the fireplace, and here there were more notices that said KEEP OFF THE GRASS, so that the gritty white paths went obediently round the edge, under the orderly trees that stood in a row like the queue[4] outside a fish shop. There were bushes in each corner and one shelter with a bench in it. Here and there brown holes in the grass, full of raked earth, waited for next year's flowers, but there were no flowers now, and the bench had been taken out of the shelter because the shelter was supposed to be a summerhouse, and you couldn't have people using a summerhouse in winter.

Robin stood by the gates and gaped, with Doggy depending limply from his mouth where he held it by one ear, between his teeth. Anthea decided that if they met anyone she knew, she would explain that Robin was only two, but very big for his age.

"Do you want to run, Robin?"

Robin shook his head.

"There's nothing to be afraid of. You can go all the way round, if you like, but you mustn't walk on the grass or pick things."

Robin nodded. It was the kind of place that he understood.

Anthea sighed. "Well, let's walk around, then."

They set off. At each corner, where the bushes were, the path diverged. One part went in front of the bushes, one part round the back of them. On the first circuit[5] Robin stumped glumly beside Anthea in front of the bushes. The second time round she felt a very faint tug at her hand. Robin wanted to go his own way.

This called for a celebration. Robin could think. Anthea crouched down on the path until they were at the same level.

"You want to walk round the back of the bushes, Robin?"

4. **queue** [kyü]: line of people waiting their turn.
5. **circuit** [sėr′ kit]: route or way around.

"Yiss," said Robin.

Robin could *talk*.

"All right, but listen." She lowered her voice to a whisper. "You must be very careful. That path is called Leopard Walk. Do you know what a leopard is?"

"Yiss."

"There are two leopards down there. They live in the bushes. One is a good leopard and the other's a bad leopard. The good leopard has black spots. The bad leopard has red spots. If you see the bad leopard, you must say, 'Die leopard die or I'll kick you in the eye,' and run like anything. Do you understand?"

Robin tugged again.

"Oh no," said Anthea. "I'm going *this* way. If you want to go down Leopard Walk, you'll have to go on your own. I'll meet you at the other end. Remember, if it's got red spots, run like mad."

Robin trotted away. The bushes were just high enough to hide him, but Anthea could see the pompom on his hat doddering along. Suddenly the pompom gathered speed, and Anthea had to run to reach the end of the bushes first.

"Did you see the bad leopard?"

"No," said Robin, but he didn't look too sure.

"Why were you running, then?"

"I just wanted to."

"You've dropped Doggy," said Anthea. Doggy lay on the path with his legs in the air, halfway down Leopard Walk.

"You get him," said Robin.

"No, *you* get him," said Anthea. "I'll wait here." Robin moved off reluctantly. She waited until he had recovered Doggy and then shouted, "I can see the bad leopard in the bushes!" Robin raced back to safety. "Did you say, 'Die leopard die or I'll kick you in the eye'?" Anthea demanded.

"No," Robin said guiltily.

"Then he'll *kill* us," said Anthea. "Come on, run. We've got to get to that tree. He can't hurt us once we're under that tree."

They stopped running under the twisted boughs of a weeping

ash. "This is a python tree," said Anthea. "Look, you can see the python wound round the trunk."

"What's a python?" said Robin, backing off.

"Oh, it's just a great big snake that squeezes people to death," said Anthea. "A python could easily eat a leopard. That's why leopards won't walk under this tree, you see, Robin."

Robin looked up. "Could it eat us?"

"Yes, but it won't if we walk on our heels." They walked on their heels to the next corner.

"Are there leopards down there?"

"No, but we must never go down there anyway. That's Poison Alley. All the trees are poisonous. They drip poison. If one bit of poison fell on your head, you'd die."

"I've got my hat on," said Robin, touching the pompom to make sure.

"It would burn right through your hat," Anthea assured him. "Right into your brains. *Fzzzzzzz.*"

They bypassed Poison Alley and walked on over the manhole cover that clanked.

"What's that?"

"That's the Fever Pit. If anyone lifts that manhole cover, they get a terrible disease. There's this terrible disease down there, Robin, and if the lid comes off, the disease will get out and people will die. I should think there's enough disease down there to kill everybody in this town. It's ever so loose, look."

"Don't lift it! Don't lift it!" Robin screamed, and ran to the shelter for safety.

"Don't go in there," yelled Anthea. "That's where the Greasy Witch lives." Robin bounced out of the shelter as though he were on elastic.

"Where's the Greasy Witch?"

"Oh, you can't see her," said Anthea, "but you can tell where she is because she smells so horrible. I think she must be somewhere about. Can't you smell her now?"

Robin sniffed the air and clasped Doggy more tightly.

Bob as Blackie Holly Roberts, 1984, oil on silver print, 20" x 24", Private collection

"And she leaves oily marks wherever she goes. Look, you can see them on the wall."

Robin looked at the wall. Someone had been very busy, if not the Greasy Witch. Anthea was glad on the whole that Robin could not read.

"The smell's getting worse, isn't it, Robin? I think we'd better go down here and then she won't find us."

"She'll see us."

"No, she won't. She can't see with her eyes because they're full of grease. She sees with her ears, but I expect they're all waxy. She's a filthy old witch, really."

They slipped down a secret-looking path that went round the back of the shelter.

"Is the Greasy Witch down here?" said Robin fearfully.

"I don't know," said Anthea. "Let's investigate." They tiptoed round the side of the shelter. The path was damp and slippery. "Filthy old witch. She's certainly *been* here," said Anthea. "I think she's gone now. I'll just have a look."

She craned her neck round the corner of the shelter. There was a sort of glade in the bushes, and in the middle was a standpipe, with a tap on top. The pipe was wrapped in canvas, like a scaly skin.

"Frightful Corner," said Anthea. Robin put his cautious head round the edge of the shelter.

"What's that?"

Anthea wondered if it could be a dragon, up on the tip of its tail and ready to strike, but on the other side of the bushes was the brick back wall of the King Street Public Conveniences, and at that moment she heard the unmistakable sound of flushing.

"It's a Lavatory Demon," she said. "Quick! We've got to get away before the water stops, or he'll have us."

They ran all the way to the gates, where they could see the church clock, and it was almost time for lunch.

Auntie Lynn fetched Robin home next morning, and three days later she was back again, striding up the path like a warrior queen going into battle, with Robin dangling from her hand and Doggy dangling from Robin's hand.

Mum took her into the front room, closing the door. Anthea sat on the stairs and listened. Auntie Lynn was in full throat and furious, so it was easy enough to hear what she had to say.

"I want a word with that young lady," said Auntie Lynn. "And I want to know what she's been telling him." Her voice dropped, and Anthea could hear only certain fateful words: "Leopards . . . poison trees . . . snakes . . . diseases!"

Mum said something very quietly that Anthea did not hear, and then Auntie Lynn turned up the volume once more.

"Won't go to bed unless I leave the door open . . . wants the light on . . . up and down to him all night . . . won't go to the bathroom on his own. He says the—the—" she hesitated. "The *toilet* demons will get him. He nearly broke his neck running downstairs this morning."

Mum spoke again, but Auntie Lynn cut in like a bandsaw.[6]

"Frightened out of his wits! He follows me everywhere."

The door opened slightly, and Anthea got ready to bolt, but it was Robin who came out, with his thumb in his mouth and circles round his eyes. Under his arm was soggy Doggy, ears chewed to nervous rags.

Robin looked up at Anthea through the banisters.

"Let's go to the park," he said.

6. **bandsaw:** saw consisting of a steel belt running over two pulleys.

JAN MARK

Jan Mark was born in 1943 in Welwyn, England. He became a teacher of art and English and did not become a "serious writer" until he was in his thirties. He says it took him that long "to develop a voice of my own." Mark has been a full-time writer since 1975. He won a fiction award for his first book, *Thunder and Lightnings.*

Mark has said that he tries to "present readers with a situation they may recognize and supplement with their own experience." He likes to drop a character into a strange environment; the story comes from the character's reactions. Two of his books are *Handles* and *At the Sign of the Dog and Rocket.* Mark has also written television plays and radio dramas.

Leslie Marmon Silko

Seeing good places
for my hands
I grab the warm parts of the cliff
and I feel the mountain as I climb.

Somewhere around here   5
yellow spotted snake is sleeping on his rock
in the sun.

So
please, I tell them
watch out,   10
don't step on the spotted yellow snake
he lives here.
The mountain is his.

Red and Yellow Cliffs Georgia O' Keeffe, 1940, oil on canvas, 24" x 36", The Metropolitan Museum of Art, New York

L E S L I E   M A R M O N   S I L K O

Leslie Marmon Silko was born in 1948 in Albuquerque, New Mexico, and grew up on the Laguna reservation. As an adult, Silko began writing novels, short stories, and poems about Native American life. One of her books is called *Ceremony*. Another book, *Storyteller*, is a collection of both poems and short stories. Silko has also written a screenplay for television.

The adventure really begins in differences—the great differences between people and animals, between the way we live now and the way we once lived, between the Mall and the Woods.

Primarily the difference between people and animals is that people use fire. People create fire, and animals don't. Oh, there are minor things—like cars and planes and all the other inventions we seem to have come up with. But in a wild state, the real difference is that we use controlled fire.

And it was in the business of fire that I came to the first of many amazements inside the woods.

It started with a campfire.

I was on a hundred-mile run in deep winter with new dogs—pups, really, just over a year old. I had gone beyond the trapping

SONG

Gary Paulsen

stage and was training new dogs for a possible attempt on the Iditarod.[1] The pups had lived in kennels, mostly. They had only been on short training runs so that almost everything they saw on this run was new to them. They had to learn to understand as they ran.

A cow in a field was a marvel and had to be investigated; it took me half an hour to get untangled from the fence. A ruffed grouse[2] that flew down the trail ahead of us had to be chased. A red squirrel took the whole team off the trail into the woods, piling into deep drifts and leaving us all upside down and packed with snow.

1. **Iditarod** [ī dit′ ə rod]: competitive dog-sled race that takes place in Alaska, usually in March.
2. **ruffed grouse** [rufd grous]: brown bird with a tuft of gleaming black feathers on each side of the neck.

from *Woodsong*   85

It was, in short, a day full of wonders for them and when night came and it was time to stop—you can really only do about twenty miles a day with young dogs—we found a soft little clearing in the spruce trees. I made beds for them and when they were fed and settled, or as settled as young dogs can get, I made a fire hole in the snow in the center of the clearing, next to the sled, and started a small fire with some dead popple.[3] It was not a cold night so the fire was very small, just enough to melt some snow and make tea. The flames didn't get over a foot high—but the effect was immediate and dramatic.

The dogs went crazy with fear. They lunged against their chains, slamming and screaming. I went to them and petted them and soothed them and at length they accepted the fire. I put their frozen blocks of meat around the edges of the flames to soften, and fed them warm meat. Then they sat and stared at the flames, the whole ring of them.

Of course they had never seen fire, or flame, in the kennel—it was all completely new to them. But the mystery was why they would automatically fear it. They had seen many new things that day, and they didn't fear anything but the fire.

And when they were over the fear of it, they were fascinated with it. I stretched my foam pad and sleeping bag out in the sled to settle in for the night. This is a complicated process. The felt liners for my shoepacs[4] had to be taken off and put down inside the bag so my body heat could dry them for the next day. My parka had to be turned inside out so all the sweat from the day could freeze and be scraped off in the morning. Any wet clothing had to be flattened and worked down into the bag to dry as well. While I was doing all this in the light from my head lamp, I let the fire die down.

Just as I started to slide into the bag one of the dogs started to sing. It was the sad song.

They have many songs and I don't know them all. There is a happy song they sing when the moon is full on the snow and they are fed and there is a rain song, which is melancholy—they don't like rain very much—and there is a song they sing when you have been

3. **popple** [pop′ əl]: poplar tree.
4. **shoepacs:** insulated boots for cold weather.

with them in the kennel and start to walk away, a come-back-and-don't-go-away sad song.

That was the song one dog had started to sing. When I turned to look at him he was staring where the fire had died down into a cup in the snow, and in a moment the rest of them had picked up the song and were wailing and moaning for the lost fire, all staring where the flames had been.

In an hour they had gone from some coded, genetic[5] fear of fire, to understanding fire, to missing it when it went away.

Cave people must have gone through this same process. I wondered how long it had taken us to understand and know fire. The pups had done it in an hour and I thought as I pulled the mummy bag up over my head and went to sleep how smart they were or perhaps how smart we weren't and thought we were.

Sometimes when they run it is not believable. And even when the run is done and obviously happened it is still not believable.

On a run once when it was the perfect temperature for running, twenty below—cold enough for the dogs to run cool, but not so bitterly cold as to freeze anything exposed—I thought I would just let them go and see what they wanted to do. I wouldn't say a word, wouldn't do anything but stand on the back of the sled—unless a bootie[6] or a quick snack was needed. I'd let them run at an easy lope. I thought I would let them go until they wanted to stop and then only run that way from then on, and they ran to some primitive instinct, coursed and ran for seventeen hours without letup.

One hundred and seventy-five miles.

And they didn't pant, weren't tired, could have done it again. I nearly froze—just a piece of meat on the back of the sled—but they ran and ran in a kind of glory and even now I can't quite believe it.

The second incident with fire was much the same—something from another world, another time. It happened, but is not quite believable.

We had run long in a day—a hundred and fifty miles—with an

5. **genetic** [je net′ ik]: inherited, inborn.
6. **bootie** [bü′ tē]: covering for the dogs' paws.

adult team in good shape. The terrain had been rough, with many moguls (mounds of snow) that made the sled bounce in the trail. I had taken a beating all day and I was whipped. I made beds and fed the dogs and built up a large fire. It had been a classic run but I was ready for sleep. It was nearly thirty below when I crawled into the sleeping bag.

I was just going to sleep, with my eyes heavy and the warmth from the fire in my face, when the dogs started an incredible uproar.

I opened my eyes and there was a deer standing right across the fire from me.

A doe. Fairly large— more than a year old—standing rigid, staring at me straight on in the face across the fire. She was absolutely petrified with terror.

At first I thought she had somehow stupidly blundered into the camp and run past the dogs to the fire.

But she hung there, staring at me, her ears rotating with the noise of the dogs around her. She did not run and still did not run and I thought she must be a medicine doe sent to me; a spirit doe come in a dream to tell me something.

Then I saw the others.

Out, perhaps thirty yards or more beyond the camp area, but close enough for the fire to shine in their eyes—the others. The wolves. There was a pack of brush wolves and they had been chasing her. I couldn't tell the number, maybe five or six; they kept moving in agitation and it was hard to pin them down, but they were clearly reluctant to let her go, although they were also clearly afraid of me and being close to me. Unlike timber wolves, brush wolves are not endangered, not protected, and are trapped heavily. We are most definitely the enemy, and they worried at seeing me.

And when I saw them I looked back at the doe and could see that she was blown. Her mouth hung open and spit smeared down both sides with some blood in it. They must have been close to getting her when she ran to the camp.

And the fire.

She must have smelled her death to make the decision she made. To run through the circle of dogs, toward the fire and the man was a mad gamble—a gamble that I wasn't a deer hunter, that the dogs weren't loose or they would have been on her like the wolves, that somehow it would be better here.

All those choices to make at a dead, frantic run with wolves pulling at her.

This time it had worked.

I sat up, half raised, afraid to move fast lest she panic and run back into the wolves. I had more wood next to the sled and I slowly put a couple of pieces on the fire and leaned back again. The wolves were very nervous now and they moved away when I put the wood on the fire, but the doe stayed nearby for a long time, so long that some of the dogs actually went back to lying down and sleeping.

She didn't relax. Her body was locked in fear and ready to fly at the slightest wrong move, but she stayed and watched me, watched the fire until the wolves were well gone and her sides were no longer heaving with hard breathing. She kept her eye on me, her ears on the dogs. Her nostrils flared as she smelled me and the fire and when she was ready— perhaps in half an hour but it seemed like much more—she wheeled, flashed her white tail at me, and disappeared.

from *Woodsong*   **89**

The dogs exploded into noise again when she ran away, then we settled back to watching the fire until sleep took us. I would have thought it all a dream except that her tracks and the tracks of the wolves were there in the morning.

Fear comes in many forms but perhaps the worst scare is the one that isn't anticipated; the one that isn't really known about until it's there. A sudden fear. The unexpected.

And again, fire played a role in it.

We have bear trouble. Because we feed processed meat to the dogs there is always the smell of meat over the kennel. In the summer it can be a bit high because the dogs like to "save" their food sometimes for a day or two or four—burying it to dig up later. We live on the edge of wilderness and consequently the meat smell brings any number of visitors from the woods.

Skunks abound, and foxes and coyotes and wolves and weasels—all predators. We once had an eagle live over the kennel for more than a week, scavenging from the dogs, and a crazy group of ravens has pretty much taken over the puppy pen. Ravens are protected by the state and they seem to know it. When I walk toward the puppy pen with the buckets of meat it's a toss-up to see who gets it—the pups or the birds. They have actually pecked the puppies away from the food pans until they have gone through and taken what they want.

Spring, when the bears come, is the worst. They have been in hibernation[7] through the winter, and they are hungry beyond caution. The meat smell draws them like flies, and we frequently have two or three around the kennel at the same time. Typically they do not bother us much—although my wife had a bear chase her from the garden to the house one morning—but they do bother the dogs.

They are so big and strong that the dogs fear them, and the bears trade on this fear to get their food. It's common to see them scare a dog into his house and take his food. Twice we have had dogs killed by rough bear swats that broke their necks—and the bears took their food.

7. **hibernation** [hī ber nā′ shən]: inactive state, like sleep, into which bears enter during the winter.

We have evolved an uneasy peace with them but there is the problem of familiarity. The first time you see a bear in the kennel it is a novelty, but when the same ones are there day after day, you wind up naming some of them (old Notch-Ear, Billy-Jo, etc.). There gets to be a too relaxed attitude. We started to treat them like pets.

A major mistake.

There was a large male around the kennel for a week or so. He had a white streak across his head which I guessed was a wound scar from some hunter—bear hunting is allowed here. He wasn't all that bad so we didn't mind him. He would frighten the dogs and take their hidden stashes now and then, but he didn't harm them and we became accustomed to him hanging around. We called him Scarhead and now and again we would joke about him as if he were one of the yard animals.

At this time we had three cats, forty-two dogs, fifteen or twenty chickens, eight ducks, nineteen large white geese, a few banty hens—one called Hawk will come up again later in the book[8]—ten fryers we'd raised from chicks and couldn't (as my wife put it) "snuff and eat," and six woods-wise goats.

The bears, strangely, didn't bother any of the yard animals. There must have been a rule, or some order to the way they lived because they would hit the kennel and steal from the dogs but leave the chickens and goats and other yard stock completely alone—although you would have had a hard time convincing the goats of this fact. The goats spent a great deal of time with their back hair up, whuffing and blowing snot at the bears—and at the dogs who would *gladly* have eaten them. The goats never really believed in the truce.

There is not a dump or landfill to take our trash to and so we separate it—organic,[9] inorganic—and deal with it ourselves. We burn the paper in a screened enclosure and it is fairly efficient, but it's impossible to get all the food particles off wrapping paper, so when it's burned the food particles burn with it.

And give off a burnt food smell.

8. **later in the book**: reference to Chapter 5 in Gary Paulsen's book *Woodsong*.
9. **organic** [ôr gan′ ik]: from plants or animals.

And nothing draws bears like burning food. It must be that they have learned to understand human dumps—where they spend a great deal of time foraging.[10] And they learn amazingly fast. In Alaska, for instance, the bears already know that the sound of a moose hunter's gun means there will be a fresh gut pile when the hunter cleans the moose. They come at a run when they hear the shot. It's often a close race to see if the hunter will get to the moose before the bears take it away. . . .

Because we're on the south edge of the wilderness area we try to wait until there is a northerly breeze before we burn so the food smell will carry south, but it doesn't always help. Sometimes bears, wolves, and other predators are already south, working the sheep farms down where it is more settled—they take a terrible toll of sheep—and we catch them on the way back through.

That's what happened one July morning.

Scarhead had been gone for two or three days and the breeze was right, so I went to burn the trash. I fired it off and went back into the house for a moment—not more than two minutes. When I came back out Scarhead was in the burn area. His tracks (directly through the tomatoes in the garden) showed he'd come from the south.

He was having a grand time. The fire didn't bother him. He was trying to reach a paw in around the edges of flame to get at whatever smelled so good. He had torn things apart quite a bit—ripped one side off the burn enclosure—and I was having a bad day and it made me mad.

I was standing across the burning fire from him and without thinking—because I was so used to him—I picked up a stick, threw it at him, and yelled, "Get out of here."

10. **foraging** [fôr´ ij ing]: searching for food.

I have made many mistakes in my life, and will probably make many more, but I hope never to throw a stick at a bear again.

In one rolling motion—the muscles seemed to move within the skin so fast that I couldn't take half a breath—he turned and came for me. Close. I could smell his breath and see the red around the sides of his eyes. Close on me he stopped and raised on his back legs and hung over me, his forelegs and paws hanging down, weaving back and forth gently as he took his time and decided whether or not to tear my head off.

I could not move, would not have time to react. I knew I had nothing to say about it. One blow would break my neck. Whether I lived or died depended on him, on his thinking, on his ideas about me—whether I was worth the bother or not.

I did not think then.

Looking back on it I don't remember having one coherent[11] thought when it was happening. All I knew was terrible menace. His eyes looked very small as he studied me. He looked down on me for what seemed hours. I did not move, did not breathe, did not think or do anything.

And he lowered.

Perhaps I was not worth the trouble. He lowered slowly and turned back to the trash and I walked backward halfway to the house and then ran—anger growing now—and took the rifle from the gun rack by the door and came back out.

He was still there, rummaging through the trash. I worked the bolt and fed a cartridge in and aimed at the place where you kill bears and began to squeeze. In raw anger, I began to take up the four pounds of pull necessary to send death into him.

And stopped.

Kill him for what?

That thought crept in.

Kill him for what?

For not killing me? For letting me know it is wrong to throw

---

11. **coherent** [kō hir′ ənt]: logical, sensible.

sticks at four-hundred-pound bears? For not hurting me, for not killing me, I should kill him? I lowered the rifle and ejected the shell and put the gun away. I hope Scarhead is still alive. For what he taught me, I hope he lives long and is very happy because I learned then—looking up at him while he made up his mind whether or not to end me—that when it is all boiled down I am nothing more and nothing less than any other animal in the woods.

GARY PAULSEN

Gary Paulsen was born in 1939 in Minneapolis, Minnesota. As a child, he lived in many different places, such as an army base in the Philippines where his father was stationed. When Paulsen grew up he tried a number of careers, including some time in the U.S. Army. He tried working as a teacher, electronics engineer, actor, farmer, rancher, truck driver, migrant farm worker, singer, sailor, and professional archer. Finally he became a full-time writer.

Paulsen has written nearly sixty books and more than two hundred short stories and articles. Most of his novels and how-to books are written for young people. Many of them, like *Woodsong, Dogsong, Tracker,* and *Hatchet,* are about experiences in the wild.

Paul Revere's

Henry Wadsworth Longfellow

Listen, my children, and you shall hear
Of the midnight ride of Paul Revere.
On the eighteenth of April, in seventy-five;
Hardly a man is now alive
Who remembers that famous day and year.   5

He said to his friend, "If the British march
By land or sea from the town tonight,
Hang a lantern aloft in the belfry[1] arch
Of the North Church tower as a signal light,—
One, if by land, and two, if by sea;   10
And I on the opposite shore will be,
Ready to ride and spread the alarm
Through every Middlesex[2] village and farm,
For the country folk to be up and to arm."

Then he said "Good night!" and with muffled oar   15
Silently rowed to the Charlestown[3] shore,
Just as the moon rose over the bay,
Where swinging wide at her moorings lay
The *Somerset*, British man-of-war;
A phantom[4] ship, with each mast and spar   20

1. **belfry** [bel′ frē]: church tower.
2. **Middlesex:** a county in Massachusetts.
3. **Charlestown:** in 1775, a town across the harbor from Boston,
   Massachusetts.
4. **phantom** [fan′ təm]: ghostly, shadowy in appearance.

Across the moon like a prison bar,
And a huge black hulk, that was magnified
By its own reflection in the tide.

Meanwhile, his friend, through alley and street,
Wanders and watches with eager ears,   25
Till in the silence around him he hears
The muster[5] of men at the barrack[6] door,
The sound of arms, and the tramp of feet,
And the measured tread of the grenadiers[7]
Marching down to their boats on the shore.   30

5. **muster:** group, gathering.
6. **barrack** [bar′ ək]: building where soldiers live.
7. **grenadiers** [gren′ ə dirz′]: soldiers in a special regiment of the
   British Army.

Horse and Rider
weather vane, c. 1900,
polychromed sheet metal,
35″ x 38″ x ½″,
Shelburne Museum,
Vermont

Then he climbed the tower of the Old North Church
By the wooden stairs, with stealthy[8] tread,
To the belfry chamber overhead,
And startled the pigeons from their perch
On the somber rafters, that round him made   35
Masses and moving shapes of shade,—
By the trembling ladder, steep and tall,
To the highest window in the wall,
Where he paused to listen and look down
A moment on the roofs of the town,   40
And the moonlight flowing over all.

Beneath, in the churchyard, lay the dead,
In their night encampment on the hill,
Wrapped in silence so deep and still
That he could hear, like a sentinel's[9] tread,   45
The watchful night wind, as it went
Creeping along from tent to tent,
And seeming to whisper, "All is well!"
A moment only he feels the spell
Of the place and the hour, and the secret dread   50
Of the lonely belfry and the dead;
For suddenly all his thoughts are bent
On a shadowy something far away,
Where the river widens to meet the bay,—
A line of black that bends and floats   55
On the rising tide, like a bridge of boats.

Meanwhile, impatient to mount and ride,
Booted and spurred, with a heavy stride
On the opposite shore walked Paul Revere.
Now he patted his horse's side,   60

8. **stealthy** [stel′ thē]: quiet and secretive.
9. **sentinel** [sen′ tə nəl]: guard.

Lantern from Old North Church
The Concord Museum, Concord, MA

Now gazed at the landscape far and near,
Then, impetuous,[10] stamped the earth,
And turned and tightened his saddle girth;[11]
But mostly he watched with eager search
The belfry tower of the Old North Church,   65
As it rose above the graves on the hill,
Lonely and spectral[12] and somber and still.
And lo! as he looks, on the belfry's height
A glimmer, and then a gleam of light!
He springs to the saddle, the bridle he turns,   70
But lingers and gazes, till full on his sight
A second lamp in the belfry burns!

A hurry of hoofs in a village street,
A shape in the moonlight, a bulk in the dark,
And beneath, from the pebbles, in passing, a spark   75
Struck out by a steed flying fearless and fleet;
That was all! And yet, through the gloom and the light,
The fate of a nation was riding that night;
And the spark struck out by that steed, in his flight,
Kindled the land into flame with its heat.   80

He has left the village and mounted the steep,
And beneath him, tranquil[13] and broad and deep,
Is the Mystic,[14] meeting the ocean tides;
And under the alders[15] that skirt its edge,
Now soft on the sand, now loud on the ledge,   85
Is heard the tramp of his steed as he rides.

10 . **impetuous** [im pech′ ü əs]: acting suddenly.
11. **girth:** strap.
12. **spectral** [spek′ trəl]: ghostly.
13. **tranquil** [trang′ kwəl]: calm, peaceful.
14. **Mystic** [mis′ tik]: river in Massachusetts.
15. **alders** [ôl′ dərz]: type of birch trees that grow in moist areas.

It was twelve by the village clock,
When he crossed the bridge into Medford town.
He heard the crowing of the cock,   90
And the barking of the farmer's dog,
And felt the damp of the river fog,
That rises after the sun goes down.

It was one by the village clock,
When he galloped into Lexington.[16]
He saw the gilded weathercock[17]   95
Swim in the moonlight as he passed,
And the meeting-house windows, blank and bare,
Gaze at him with a spectral glare,
As if they already stood aghast[18]
At the bloody work they would look upon.   100

It was two by the village clock,
When he came to the bridge in Concord town.
He heard the bleating of the flock,
And the twitter of birds among the trees,
And felt the breath of the morning breeze   105
Blowing over the meadows brown.
And one was safe and asleep in his bed
Who at the bridge would be first to fall,
Who that day would be lying dead,
Pierced by a British musket ball.   110

16. **Lexington:** town in Massachusetts where the first
    battle of the American Revolution was fought on
    April 19, 1775.
17. **weathercock:** weather vane in the shape of a rooster.
18. **aghast** [ə gast′]: surprised, amazed.

Bootmaker's trade sign   c. 1900,
wood painted, 34 1/2″ x 9″ x 21″,
Shelburne Museum, Vermont

You know the rest. In the books you have read,
How the British Regulars[19] fired and fled,—
How the farmers gave them ball for ball,
From behind each fence and farmyard wall,
Chasing the redcoats[20] down the lane,   115
Then crossing the fields to emerge again
Under the trees at the turn of the road,
And only pausing to fire and load.

So through the night rode Paul Revere;
And so through the night went his cry of alarm   120
To every Middlesex village and farm,—
A cry of defiance and not of fear,
A voice in the darkness, a knock at the door,
And a word that shall echo forevermore!
For, borne on the night wind of the past,   125
Through all our history, to the last,
In the hour of darkness and peril and need,
The people will waken and listen to hear
The hurrying hoof-beats of that steed,
And the midnight message of Paul Revere.   130

19. **British Regulars:** members of the permanent army of Great Britain.
20. **redcoats:** British soldiers.

HENRY WADSWORTH
LONGFELLOW

Henry Wadsworth Longfellow [1807-1882] was
born in Portland, Maine. He attended Harvard
University and then studied and traveled in Europe.
Longfellow published his first poems while in college. He lived for many
years in Boston, Massachusetts.

Longfellow became known as a poet of adventure and patriotism.
His poem "The Song of Hiawatha" became a classic. Longfellow was also
concerned with social injustice. In 1842, well before the Civil War,
Longfellow spoke out about slavery in his book *Poems on Slavery*.

Asking Big Questions About the Literature

What makes an adventure?

Setting

The time and place in which the action of a story occurs is called the **setting.** A good adventure often takes place in a dangerous or unfamiliar setting, such as a mountain top or a space shuttle. In your journal, write a paragraph for each literature selection you have read, explaining why the setting is important for the adventure. (*See "Setting" on page 118.*)

Write a
GREETING CARD

Imagine that you're on one of the adventures that you've read about in the literature selections. Write a greeting card to the folks back home, explaining what makes your adventure different from an ordinary, quiet vacation.

MAKE AN ADVENTURE CHART

Make a chart like the one below, showing what makes an adventure in each selection that you've read. When you've finished, use your chart to write a short essay describing the features of a typical adventure story.

Literature Selection	Features of Adventure
"The Mountain That Refused to Be Climbed"	a challenging goal dangerous terrain adventurer pursuing a dream

How do people react to their adventures?

COMPARING
Adventures

Make a chart like the one below, showing how different characters in the selections you have read react to their adventures. Then use your chart to help you write a short essay comparing the characters' reactions.

Write a
DIARY ENTRY

Imagine that you are a character in one of the literature selections you've read. How do you feel about the adventure you're on? Write a diary entry from that character's point of view. Describe your reactions to the story's events.

Selection	Type of Adventure	Character	Reaction

LITERATURE STUDY

Character

A **character** is a person or an animal that participates in the action of a work of literature. Choose a character from a literature selection you've read in this unit. Then write an adventure story of your own that features the same character. Show how he or she would react to a very different situation. (*See "Character" on page 119.*)

Asking Big Questions About the Literature

What are adventurers like?

LITERATURE STUDY

Character

A good writer will reveal the personality of a **character** through his or her thoughts, words, and deeds. If you were making one of the selections you've read into a movie, which actor or actress would you cast as the adventurer? Write this person a letter explaining why you think he or she would be good for the role. (See "Character" on page 119.)

Write a Magazine
ARTICLE

Write a magazine cover story called "Adventurer of the Year." Choose a character from a literature selection you've read. Write an article about this character in which you describe the character's achievements and personality.

A Map of Qualities

In a group, discuss adventurers you've read about. Write a list of their qualities in the center of a journal page. Then make a Quality Map like the one below by surrounding the list with the circled names of adventurers you read about in this unit. Draw a line from each quality to the appropriate character or characters. Then write a character profile of your favorite adventurer.

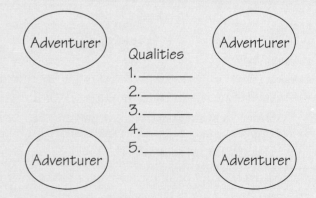

Adventurer

Adventurer

Qualities
1. _____
2. _____
3. _____
4. _____
5. _____

Adventurer

Adventurer

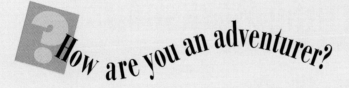

How are you an adventurer?

Self-Evaluation Chart

Think of the adventurers in the selections you've read. What qualities made them good adventurers? Do you share any of these qualities? Make a self-evaluation chart like the one below. List your good qualities. Beside each quality, describe the time when this quality helped you in a challenging situation.

Good Quality	When It Helped
_____	_____
_____	_____
_____	_____

LITERATURE STUDY

Setting

The **setting**—the time and place in which a story's action occurs—often determines the plot of an adventure. Look through the fiction selections in this unit for stories in which the setting affected the plot. Then think of a time when your surroundings presented you with a challenge. Show how you faced this challenge by writing a short adventure story, with yourself as the main character. Include a good description of the setting. (*See "Setting" on page 118.*)

News Story About You

Many adventurers are trailblazers. Look through the selections in this unit for examples of people who were the first in the world to achieve some goal. Now imagine yourself achieving something unique. Then write a news article or broadcast reporting your achievement. Share your article or broadcast with classmates.

NOW Choose a Project!

Three projects involving adventure are described on the following pages. Which one is for you?

PROJECT 1

Writing Workshop

WRITING A TRAVEL BROCHURE

If you could lead an expedition, where would you go? What would you do? In this project, you'll plan the adventure of a lifetime. After you've researched your destination, you'll publish a travel brochure to present to your **audience** of classmates. The **purpose** of your brochure will be to present a travel plan so exciting that your classmates will want to join you in your adventure.

Prewriting
GETTING STARTED

First collect some travel brochures from local travel agencies or the library. Study them to see how they are set up. To help you choose a destination, start with some freewriting in your journal. Is there some place that you've always wanted to visit? Brainstorm a list of places. Use a globe or atlas in the library to help you with your list. Write down the names of interesting places you find in world atlases, encyclopedias, travel books, and magazines. Ask yourself these questions to limit your topic:

- Is it a place where there will be lots of things to do?
- Will we be able to get around easily?
- Will the climate be right?

Then choose a destination.

Researching
YOUR DESTINATION

Now research your destination. Again, use the library to gather information. Take notes as you find the answers to these questions:

- What will the weather be like?
- What will the local food be like?
- What are the main geographic features?
- What are the main points of interest?
- What plants and animals will we find?

To take notes, write your question at the top of an index card or sheet of paper. Below the question, write the information and its source. You'll use these cards when you organize your information into the different paragraphs of your travel brochure.

When you have gathered information about your destination, ask yourself these questions and write the answers in your journal.

- Will we be staying in one place or traveling around?
- How will we travel and where will we stay?
- What risks and challenges will we face?
- What will we need to take with us?

Show your list of questions to one or more classmates. Is there anything else they'd like to know? Consider their suggestions. Think about your *itinerary*, or the schedule you will follow during your trip.

Drafting
YOUR TRAVEL BROCHURE

Before you draft your travel brochure, remember both your **purpose**—to make your destination sound appealing to other travelers—and your **audience**.

- Write an introduction that will catch your audience's attention. For example, Luke Hohreiter, a student writer, asks a question to introduce his travel guide on pages 110-111. "Are you ready for a vacation?" Who wouldn't answer "Yes!"

- Use each index card that you filled out during your research phase to write a paragraph on a different subject. Write separate paragraphs on the geography, the weather, and the main points of interest of your destination. Notice that Luke has written separate paragraphs on Costa Rica's climate, geography, food, and tourist attractions.

- Draft a conclusion that will make readers start packing! Luke writes that "Costa Rica has all the characteristics of the perfect getaway at half the price of any other vacation of the same quality." Who could ask for more?

- Include an itinerary, if you have one. Under the headings Day 1, Day 2, and so on, outline the schedule of your expedition. Don't forget to work in traveling time to and from the country you've chosen.

Revising

YOUR TRAVEL BROCHURE

You've finished your first draft. Is it complete? Is it clear? Is it exciting? Does it have all the information that a potential traveler might need? Show it to a classmate or your writing group. Would it persuade others to join you on this adventure? Look it over carefully yourself, too. Get more information, make changes, and reorganize your paragraphs if necessary. Do whatever you need to do to make your expedition sound absolutely terrific.

Editing

YOUR TRAVEL BROCHURE

After you've revised your draft, work with a partner or writing group to edit your travel brochure. Read one another's guides and check for errors in grammar, punctuation, and spelling. Correct your errors and make a publishable copy of your brochure. Remember that a good editing job now will mean happy travelers later.

Publishing

YOUR TRAVEL BROCHURE

Look through magazines and books for pictures of your destination. If you can't cut them out, xerox them and arrange them next to the text of your travel brochure. Then present your guide to the class or combine your brochures into a travel book.

Writing Workshop

TRAVEL BROCHURE
by Luke Hohreiter
West Palm Beach, Florida

Are you ready for a vacation? Do you want to enjoy a week of blissful leisure in a tropical paradise, relaxing on the beach, hiking along a steep mountain trail, or even white water rafting down a swift, pristine river? If this is the kind of adventure you are looking for, Costa Rica is the place for you. Its pleasant climate and peaceful atmosphere, as well as its exotic beauty, provide the perfect escape from your hectic daily schedule.

Costa Rica's climate is wet most of the year and the temperature depends on the altitude. In some parts it rains about 300 days out of the year, but it also has a dry season, so plan accordingly. Because altitude determines the temperature, you could take a hike in the mountains and be greeted by a gentle snow flurry or relax on the beach while sipping a cold drink and basking in the sun. Although over the course of your vacation you will experience all of these diverse climates, the beginning of your adventure will take place in an area with weather so beautiful it is called the place of "Eternal Spring." This region is known as the Central Valley and consists of San José, Heredia, Alajuela, and Cartago.

Costa Rica has some of the most diverse geography in the world. Central Costa Rica consists mostly of dense jungles except for the Central Valley which rests on a large plateau. As you travel to the east and west, you will find great mountain ranges that stretch across

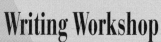

the country. The mountains eventually slope into foothills and then into miles and miles of tropical savannahs. From there, savannahs melt away into white, sandy beaches which are excellent fishing grounds.

If food is high on your agenda, you won't be disappointed with the local entrees. In the countryside you may find more traditional cuisine, which is often vegetarian. In San José, however, you will find "International Cuisine," a combination of North American and European dishes. The main course of each meal is usually some type of meat, either beef, chicken, or fish, with rice and cabbage on the side. A traditional and very common dish is casado, which is a serving of meat, usually beef, and rice, beans, and cabbage. After your meal, you might have cajeta, which is a dessert dish that consists of heavy milk fudge.

After spending a night in one of Costa Rica's lovely hotels, a visit to one of its major tourist attractions—a world-renowned national park—would be most appealing. One of the most well-known and popular parks among tourists is Santa Rosa. This park is known for its scenic hiking trails and its many species of exotic birds.

As you can see, Costa Rica has all the characteristics of the perfect getaway at half the price of any other vacation of the same quality. For these reasons and many more, it would be the best choice for a fun and interesting place to visit.

Itinerary

Day One

Depart from Miami
Arrive in San José
Check into hotel
Have dinner at a local restaurant

Day Two

Tour of San José
Lunch at hotel
Tour of nearby towns

Day Three

Travel to the coast by bus
Check into hotel and head to local river
for white-water rafting

Cooperative Learning

PLANNING A TREASURE HUNT

Have you ever dreamed of searching for lost treasure? In this project, you and a group of classmates will plan a treasure hunt for charity or just for fun. It will be an "obstacle course" with a trail of clues leading to a hidden treasure.

The PROCESS

First, decide on your main purpose. Will it be for entertainment or charity? Then select the "hunters"—the people who'll search for the hidden treasure. Finally decide what the treasure itself will be.

Organize your project into steps. First, you need to agree on the main steps: researching your theme, finding a place and time for the hunt, mapping out the hunt, creating clues, and so on. It may help to create a Job Sequence Chain like the one shown.

Then come up with a theme for your adventure. It could be based on a famous historical adventure or a scientific discovery. For example, if you choose an Egyptian theme, you could bury copies of objects belonging to the Pharaoh. Divide into teams studying history, science, and other subjects. Discuss the team's findings and choose a theme for your hunt.

Now form task teams. Each team will work to complete one major step, while keeping in close contact with the other teams. Remember that one team's decision may affect another team's plan. The map team and the clue team especially will have to work closely together.

Job Sequence Chain

Step One: Researching the theme

Step Two

Step Three — Step Four — Step Five — Step Six: The Hunt

Within each team, make a work plan like the one below that shows each person's responsibility.

Team Member	Responsibility
Bill	
Sue	
Chris	

When the teams have completed their tasks, meet together as a group and finalize your plan.

The HUNT

Write your clues and plant them. Put the treasure in its hiding place. Explain the theme to the hunters before they begin their search. Then let the game begin!

TREASURE MAP

SCHOOL

CLUES to find King Tut's Treasure

1. One half of the way between the boy's right index finger and the tip of the dark palm tree leaf, go due North for two feet.

2. Three quarters of the way between this point and the bottom right corner of the pyramid go West for four feet.

3. When you get to this point, go South for three feet and start digging.

by Michael Maloney, Grade 7, Bath, Maine

⊢—⊣ = 1 foot

Helping Your Community

CELEBRATING LOCAL ADVENTURERS

If you think adventurers are found only in movies and books, look around you! Your community is full of adventurers. In this project, you'll work with a partner or group to put together a tribute to the adventurers in your community.

The SEARCH

First, decide on the form your tribute will take. Could you make a book or assemble a "Wall of Adventurers" in your school or community? Could you present a slide show or make a video?

Then decide whether to create a profile of adventurers from your school, neighborhood, or town. Start your search for adventurers by asking yourself the Big Question "What are adventurers like?"

To gather information on adventurers in your school, scan back issues of school publications. For information on adventurers in your town, look at newspapers and books on local history. Make a list of community adventurers.

Choose people from the list. Research historical figures in the library. Contact any living adventurers and interview them directly. Use the following questions to help you get the information you need.

- What did the adventurer do?
- What is the adventurer's background?
- What does the adventurer feel about his or her achievement?

Marc Freedman, round-the-world cyclist, in front of signs at Red Center, Australia

Now write a short piece of biographical information about each adventurer. Collect photographs of the adventurers as well. Form a design group that will arrange the information for presentation.

The
PRESENTATION

Decide when and where to present your project. Are there other organizations that might be interested in your project? You may find many others who would be interested in your tribute to the adventurers in your community.

These photographs were taken during Marc Freedman's round-the-world bicycling trip. During his eight-year journey, Marc spent five years on the road and three years working in various countries along the way.

Marc Freedman with Guatemalan children

Marc Freedman resting on a rock in Zimbabwe, Africa

Melissa Johnson at South Island, New Zealand

Putting It All Together

What Have You Learned About Adventures?

Now that your adventures in this unit are over, consider how your ideas on this theme have changed. You've read and thought about a world of exciting challenges. Show what you learned about adventures by writing an adventure story in which you are the main character.

YOUR EXCELLENT ADVENTURE

Prewriting and Drafting   Look back at all the writing you did for this unit—in your journal, in response to your reading, and in the Writing Workshop. Does any of the material help you with ideas for a fantastic adventure of your own? For example, if you worked on the Writing Workshop, you could live out your travel plan in your imagination. Brainstorm ideas for a fabulous adventure that takes place anywhere in the universe. It could take place under the sea, on another planet, or even during another period of history. Whatever you choose as the setting of your story, just remember that this story will be about *you*.

Now draft your story. You could begin by describing the setting, with a quotation from yourself as the main character. Fill your plot with challenges that must be overcome. Let the story's events build to an exciting conclusion. Remember to include dialogue.

Revising and Editing   Work with a partner or writing group. Exchange stories and ask for comments on and advice about the content of your writing. Have your partner or group check your errors in grammar, spelling, and punctuation.

Publishing   Rewrite your story neatly and give it a title. Post it on a class bulletin board so that your classmates can read it. If you like, you could gather all your classmates' stories into a book entitled *Our Excellent Adventures*.

Evaluating Your Work

Think Back About the Big Questions

Think about the Big Questions on pages 10-11. Discuss your thoughts with a partner, especially your thoughts about questions that still seem hard to answer. Compare your ideas now with your ideas when you started this unit. Record your current thoughts in your journal.

Think Back About Your Work

Now think about the whole unit. What did you do? How did you do? To evaluate your work, including your reading, your writing, your activities, and your project, write a note to your teacher. Explain what you've done during this unit and what you've learned. Use the following questions to help you write your note.

- Which literature selections in this unit did you like the most? Why?
- What was your favorite activity in this unit? Why?
- What was your least favorite activity? Why?
- If you were to do your project again, what parts would you do the same way? What parts would you do differently?
- What did you learn as you worked on your project or projects?
- What have you learned in this unit about adventure and adventurers?
- How would you rate your work in this unit? Use the following scale and give at least three reasons for your rating.

1 = Outstanding	3 = Fair
2 = Good	4 = Not as good as it could have been

SETTING

What Is Setting?

Setting is the time and place in which the action of a story or a poem occurs. The setting may be described at the beginning of the story, or it may be presented through details that appear as the story unfolds. In an adventure story, the setting often has an important role in the plot. In "The Mountain That Refused to Be Climbed," for example, the setting is one reason why the adventure takes place. Because of this, the setting is described in great detail. We learn that the mountain "is a moving mass of ice. Anyone climbing it may encounter dangerous crevasses—deep fissures that drop suddenly into abysses—and snow avalanches that unexpectedly thunder down."

Rewriting a Setting   Choose a character from a literature selection that you've read. Write an adventure story in which the character wakes up in an entirely different setting. How would the setting affect the outcome of the plot? How would the character react to this new setting, given what you know about the character from the selection you've read?

Comparing Settings   Choose two selections that you've read in this unit that have very different settings. Then write a short essay comparing how the adventurers in the selections react to the settings. What does each character's reaction tell you about that character's personality?

What Is Character?

A **character** is a person or an animal that participates in the action of a work of literature. To make characters believable, authors give them personality traits and describe their physical appearance. A good writer will try to visualize a character in great detail and allow the character's personality to express itself through his or her thoughts, words, and actions. For example, in "The True Confessions of Charlotte Doyle" we learn a great deal about Charlotte's courage and determination through her thoughts and movements as she struggles up the ship's mast, proving that she is as brave as any sailor.

A Talk Show   Choose an adventurous character from a literature selection you've read. With a partner, conduct an interview between this character and a televison talk show host. The talk show host should ask the character about the events in the literature selection as if they actually happened. The person who plays the character should assume his or her personality as if the events actually happened. Perform your interview in front of the class.

Creating a Character   Create a female or male super adventurer who has the good qualities of all the adventurers you've read about. Then write the opening paragraphs of a story about this character. Provide the super adventurer with some challenge that she or he must overcome. Show what the character is like through his or her thoughts, words, and actions.

GLOSSARY OF LITERARY TERMS

A

alliteration   Repetition of the first sound—usually a consonant sound—in several words of a sentence or a line of poetry.

allusion   An author's indirect reference to someone or something that is presumed to be familiar to the reader.

anecdote   A short narrative about an interesting or a humorous event, usually in the life of a person.

antagonist   The person or force opposing the protagonist, or main character in a literary work. [See also *protagonist*.]

autobiography   A person's written account of his or her own life.

B

ballad   A poem, often a song, that tells a story in simple verse.

biography   An account of a person's life, written by another person.

blank verse   Unrhymed poetry.

C

character   A person or an animal that participates in the action of a work of literature. A *dynamic character* is one whose thoughts, feelings, and actions are changeable and lifelike; a *static character* always remains the same. [See also *protagonist, antagonist*.]

characterization   The creation of characters through the characters' use of language and through descriptions of their appearance, thoughts, emotions, and actions. [See also *character*.]

chronology   An arrangement of events in the order in which they happen.

cliché   An overused expression that is trite rather than meaningful.

climax   The highest point of tension in the plot of a work of literature. [See also *plot*.]

comedy   An amusing play that has a happy ending.

conclusion   The final part or ending of a piece of literature.

concrete poem   A poem arranged on the page so that its punctuation, letters, and lines make the shape of the subject of the poem.

conflict   A problem that confronts the characters in a piece of literature. The conflict may be *internal* (a character's struggle within himself or herself) or *external* (a character's struggle against nature, another person, or society). [See also *plot*.]

context   The general sense of words that helps readers to understand the meaning of unfamiliar words and phrases in a piece of writing.

D

description   An author's use of words to give the reader or listener a mental picture, an impression, or an understanding of a person, place, thing, event, or idea.

dialect   A form of speech spoken by people in a particular group or geographical region that differs in vocabulary, grammar, and pronunciation from the standard language.

dialogue   The spoken words and conversation of characters in a work of literature.

drama   A play that is performed before an audience according to stage directions and using dialogue. Classical drama has two genres: *tragedy* and *comedy*. Modern drama includes *melodrama, satire, theater of the absurd,* and *pantomime*. [See also *comedy, play,* and *tragedy*.]

dramatic poetry   A play written in the form of poetry.

E

epic   A long narrative poem—written in a formal style and meant to be read aloud—that relates the adventures and experiences of one or more great heroes or heroines.

essay   Personal nonfiction writing about a particular subject that is important to the writer.

excerpt   A passage from a larger work that has been taken out of its context to be used for a special purpose.

exposition   Writing that explains, analyzes, or defines.

extended metaphor   An elaborately drawn out metaphor. [See also *metaphor*.]

F

fable   A short, simple story whose purpose is to teach a lesson, usually with animal characters who talk and act like people.

fantasy   Imaginative fiction about unrealistic characters, places, and events.

fiction   Literature, including the short story and the novel, that tells about imaginary people and events.

figurative language
Language used to express ideas through figures of speech: descriptions that aren't meant to be taken literally. Types of figurative language include *simile, metaphor, extended metaphor, hyperbole,* and *personification*.

figure of speech   A type of figurative language, not meant to be taken literally, that expresses something in such a way that it brings the thing to life in the reader's or listener's imagination. [See also *figurative language*.]

flashback   A break in a story's action that relates a past happening in order to give the reader background information about a present action in the story.

folktale   A story that has been passed along from storyteller to storyteller for generations. Kinds of folktales include *tall tales, fairy tales, fables, legends,* and *myths*.

foreshadowing   The use of clues to create suspense by giving the reader or audience hints of events to come.

free verse   Poetry that has no formal rhyme scheme or metrical pattern.

G

genre   A major category of art. The three major literary genres are poetry, prose, and drama.

H

haiku   A three-line Japanese verse form. In most haiku, the first and third lines have five syllables, while the second line has seven. The

traditional haiku describes a complicated feeling or thought in simple language through a single image.

hero/heroine   The main character in a work of literature. In heroic literature, the hero or heroine is a particularly brave, noble, or clever person whose achievements are unusual and important. [See also *character*.]

heroic age   The historical period in western civilization—from about 800 B.C. through A.D. 200—during which most works of heroic literature, such as myths and epics, were created in ancient Greece and Rome.

hubris   Arrogance or excessive pride leading to mistakes; the character flaw in a hero of classical tragedy.

hyperbole   An obvious exaggeration used for emphasis. [See also *figurative language*.]

I

idiom   An expression whose meaning cannot be understood from the ordinary meaning of the words. For example, *It's raining cats and dogs*.

imagery   The words and phrases in writing that appeal to the senses of sight, hearing, taste, touch, and smell.

irony An effect created by a sharp contrast between what is expected and what is real. An *ironic twist* in a plot is an event that is the complete opposite of what the characters have been hoping or expecting will happen. An *ironic statement* declares the opposite of the speaker's literal meaning.

J

jargon Words and phrases used by a group of people who share the same profession or special interests in order to refer to technical things or processes with which they are familiar. In general, jargon is any terminology that sounds unclear, overused, or pretentious.

L

legend A famous folktale about heroic actions, passed along by word of mouth from generation to generation. The legend may have begun as a factual account of real people and events but has become mostly or completely fictitious.

limerick A form of light verse, or humorous poetry, written in one five-line stanza with a regular scheme of rhyme and meter.

literature The branch of art that is expressed in written language and includes all written genres.

lyric poem A short poem that expresses personal feelings and thoughts in a musical way. Originally, lyrics were the words of songs that were sung to music played on the lyre, a stringed instrument invented by the ancient Greeks.

M

metamorphosis The transformation of one thing, or being, into another completely different thing or being, such as a caterpillar's change into a butterfly.

metaphor Figurative language in which one thing is said to be another thing. [See also *figurative language*.]

meter The pattern of rhythm in lines of poetry. The most common meter, in poetry written in English, is iambic pentameter, that is, a verse having five metrical feet, each foot of verse having two syllables, an unaccented one followed by an accented one.

mood The feeling or atmosphere that a reader senses while reading or listening to a work of literature.

motivation A character's reasons for doing, thinking, feeling, or saying something. Sometimes an author will make a character's motivation obvious from the beginning. In realistic fiction and drama, however, a character's motivation may be so complicated that the reader discovers it gradually, by studying the character's thoughts, feelings, and behavior.

myth A story, passed along by word of mouth for generations, about the actions of gods and goddesses or superhuman heroes and heroines. Most myths were first told to explain the origins of natural things or to justify the social rules and customs of a particular society.

N

narration The process of telling a story. For both fiction and nonfiction, there are two main kinds of narration, based on whether the story is told from a first-person or third-person point of view. [See also *point of view*.]

narrative poem A poem that tells a story containing the basic literary ingredients of fiction: character, setting, and plot.

narrator The person, or voice, that tells a story. [See also *point of view, voice*.]

nonfiction Prose that is factually true and is about real people, events, and places.

nonstandard English
Versions of English, such as slang and dialects, that use pronunciation, vocabulary, idiomatic expressions, grammar, and punctuation that differ from the accepted "correct" constructions of English.

novel   A long work of narrative prose fiction. A novel contains narration, a setting or settings, characters, dialogue, and a more complicated plot than a short story.

O

onomatopoeia   The technique of using words that imitate the sounds they describe, such as *hiss, buzz,* and *splash.*

oral tradition   Stories, poems, and songs that have been kept alive by being told, recited, and sung by people over many generations. Since the works were not originally written, they often have many different versions.

P

parable   A brief story—similar to a fable, but about people—that describes an ordinary situation and concludes with a short moral or lesson to be learned.

personification   Figurative language in which an animal, an object, or an idea is given human characteristics. [See also *figurative language*.]

persuasion   A type of speech or writing whose purpose is to convince people that something is true or important.

play   A work of dramatic literature written for performance by actors before an audience. In classical or traditional drama, a play is divided into five acts, each containing a number of scenes. Each act represents a distinct phase in the development of the plot. Modern plays often have only one act and one scene.

playwright   The author of a play.

plot   The sequence of actions and events in fiction or drama. A traditional plot has at least three parts: the *rising action,* leading up to a turning point that affects the main character; the *climax,* the turning point or moment of greatest intensity or interest; and the *falling action,* leading away from the conflict, or resolving it.

poetry   Language selected and arranged in order to say something in a compressed or nonliteral way. Modern poetry may or may not use many of the traditional poetic techniques that include *meter, rhyme, alliteration, figurative language, symbolism,* and *specific verse forms.*

point of view   The perspective from which a writer tells a story. *First-person* narrators tell the story from their own point of view, using pronouns such as *I* or *me. Third-person* narrators, using pronouns such as *he, she,* or *them,* may be *omniscient* (knowing everything about all characters), or *limited* (taking the point of view of one character). [See also *narration.*]

propaganda   Information or ideas that may or may not be true, but are spread as though they are true, in order to persuade people to do or believe something.

prose   The ordinary form of written and spoken language used to create fiction, nonfiction, and most drama.

protagonist   The main character of a literary work. [See also *character* and *characterization.*]

R

refrain   A line or group of lines that is repeated, usually at the end of each verse, in a poem or a song.

repetition   The use of the same formal element more than once in a literary work, for emphasis or in order to achieve another desired effect.

resolution   The falling action in fiction or drama,

including all of the developments that follow the climax and show that the story's conflict is over. [See also *plot*.]

rhyme scheme   A repeated pattern of similar sounds, usually found at the ends of lines of poetry or poetic drama.

rhythm   In poetry, the measured recurrence of accented and unaccented syllables in a particular pattern. [See also *meter*.]

S

scene   The time, place, and circumstances of a play or a story. In a play, a scene is a section of an act. [See also *play*.]

science fiction   Fantasy literature set in an imaginary future, with details and situations that are designed to seem scientifically possible.

setting   The time and place of a work of literature.

short story   Narrative prose fiction that is shorter and has a less complicated plot than a novel. A short story contains narration, at least one setting, at least one character, and usually some dialogue.

simile   Figurative language that compares two unlike things, introduced by the words "like" or "as." [See also *figurative language*.]

soliloquy   In a play, a short speech spoken by a single character when he or she is alone on the stage. A soliloquy usually expresses the character's innermost thoughts and feelings, when he or she thinks no other characters can hear.

sonnet   A poem written in one stanza, using fourteen lines of iambic pentameter. [See also *meter*.]

speaker   In poetry, the individual whose voice seems to be speaking the lines. [See also *narration, voice*.]

stage directions   The directions, written by the playwright, to tell the director, actors, and theater technicians how a play should be dramatized. Stage directions may specify such things as how the setting should appear in each scene, how the actors should deliver their lines, when the stage curtain should rise and fall, how stage lights should be used, where on the stage the actors should be during the action, and when sound effects should be used.

stanza   A group of lines in poetry set apart by blank lines before and after the group; a poetic verse.

style   The distinctive way in which an author composes a

work of literature in written or spoken language.

suspense   An effect created by authors of various types of fiction and drama, especially adventure and mystery, to heighten interest in the story.

symbol   An image, person, place, or thing that is used to express the idea of something else.

T

tall tale   A kind of folk tale, or legend, that exaggerates the characteristics of its hero or heroine.

theme   The main idea or underlying subject of a work of literature.

tone   The attitude that a work of literature expresses to the reader through its style.

tragedy   In classical drama, a tragedy depicts a noble hero or heroine who makes a mistake of judgment that has disastrous consequences.

V

verse   A stanza in a poem. Also, a synonym for poetry as a genre. [See also *stanza*.]

voice   The narrator or the person who relates the action of a piece of literature. [See also *speaker*.]

ACKNOWLEDGMENTS

Grateful acknowledgment is made for permission to reprint the following copyrighted material.

"The Mountain That Refused to Be Climbed" from *Living Dangerously: American Women Who Risked Their Lives for Adventure*. Copyright © 1991 by Doreen Rappaport. By permission of HarperCollins Publishers.

From "Burning" by Gary Snyder from *Myths and Texts*. Copyright © 1978 by Gary Snyder. Reprinted by permission of New Directions Publishing Corp.

"The Stars, My Goal: Guion Stewart Bluford, Jr." by Jim Haskins from *Against All Opposition: Black Explorers in America*. Copyright © 1992 by Jim Haskins. Used with permission of Walker Publishing Company, 720 Fifth Avenue, New York, NY 10019, 1-800-289-2553.

"What I Want to Be When I Grow Up" by Martha Brooks from *Paradise Cafe and Other Stories*. Copyright © 1988 by Martha Brooks. By permission of Little, Brown and Company.

"When in Reality" by Maurice Kenny from *Words in the Blood: Contemporary Indian Writers of North and South America*, edited by Jamake Highwater. Copyright ©1984 by Jamake Highwater.

From *The True Confessions of Charlotte Doyle* by Avi. Copyright © 1990 by Avi. Used with permission of Orchard Books, New York.

"The Kitchen Knight" by Margaret Hodges. Text copyright © 1990 by Margaret Hodges. All rights reserved. Reprinted by permission of Holiday House.

"The Getaway" by John Savage is reprinted from the *Saturday Evening Post*, May 7, 1966, Issue No. 10.

"Nothing to Be Afraid Of" by Jan Mark. Copyright © 1991 by Jan Mark. By permission of HarperCollins Publishers.

"The Time We Climbed Snake Mountain" by Leslie Marmon Silko from *StoryTeller*. Copyright © 1981 by Leslie Marmon Silko. By permission of the author.

From *Woodsong* by Gary Paulsen, copyright © 1990 by Gary Paulsen. By permission of Bradbury Press, an Affiliate of Macmillan, Inc.

ILLUSTRATION

8 Maze by Dave Shepherd.

PHOTOGRAPHY

4 *l* Richard Haynes/©D.C. Heath; *r* Sarah Putnam/©D.C. Heath; 5 Universitätsbibliothek Heidelberg, Germany; 6 Julie Bidwell/©D.C. Heath; 8-9 Brian Seed/Tony Stone Images; 10 *t* Sarah Putnam/©D.C. Heath; *b* Richard Haynes/©D.C. Heath; 11 *t* John Owens/©D.C. Heath; *c* Jim Whitmer/Stock Boston; *b* Sarah Putnam/©D.C. Heath; 12 *inset* A Search for the Apex of America by Annie S. Peck, New York, Dodd, Mead and Company, 1911. General Research Division, New York Public Library Astor, Lenox and Tilden Foundations; 12-13 Rob Crandall/The Image Works; 16-17, *background*, 20-21 *background*, 21, 23 A Search for the Apex of America by Annie S. Peck, New York, Dodd, Mead and Company, 1911. General Research Division, New York Public Library Astor, Lenox and Tilden Foundations; 25 Courtesy of HarperCollins Publishers; 26-27 Albright-Knox Art Gallery, Buffalo, NY. George B. and Jenny R. Mathews Fund, 1981; 27 *l* Virginia Schedhler. Courtesy of New Directions Corp.; 28 *inset* Courtesy of Abbeville Press; 28-35 Navaswan/FPG International; 29 *insets* Courtesy of Abbeville Press; 31 *inset* Sovfoto; 33, 34-35 *c* NASA; 37 Private Collection, courtesy of Marlborough Gallery. ©Richard Estes/VAGA, New York, 1995. Photo courtesy of the Allan Stone Gallery, New York; 40 The Museum of Modern Art, New York, Philip Johnson Fund. ©George Segal/VAGA, NY, 1995; 43 Courtesy of Little Brown and Company; 44 *inset* Courtesy of White Pine Press; 44-45 Computer photo illustration by Jim Carroll; 46 *inset* G. Brimacombe/The Image Bank; 46-51 Superstock; 51 *inset* Tibor Bognar/The Stock Market; 52-55 Superstock; 55 *inset* DRS Productions/Steve Mason/The Stock Market; 56-57 Superstock; 58, 63, 66 Universitätsbibliothek Heidelberg, Germany; 67 Courtesy of Holiday House; 68-71 Jan Halaska/Photo Researchers; 72 Courtesy of Rex Lau; 79 ©Holly Roberts, Collection of Pamela Portwood and Mark Taylor. Courtesy Etherton Stern Gallery, Tuscon, AZ; 81 Courtesy of HarperCollins Publishers; 83 *t* The Metropolitan Museum of Art, Alfred Stieglitz Collection. Bequest of Georgia O'Keeffe, 1986. (1987.377.4); *b* Gus Nitsche; 84-85 Ken Graham/AllStock; 88 Stephen Krasemann/AllStock; 93 Darrell Gulin/AllStock; 95 Courtesy of Penguin USA; 96-97 Shelburne Museum, Shelburne, VT. Photo by Ken Burris; 98-99 Photograph courtesy of the Concord Museum, Concord, MA; 100 Shelburne Museum, Shelburne, VT. Photo by Ken Burris; 101 *inset* Historical Pictures/Stock Montage, Inc.; 103 Nancy Sheehan/©D.C. Heath; 106 *t* Elizabeth Hamlin/Stock Boston; *b* David J. Sams/Stock Boston; 107 Michael Fogden/DRK; 109 Alon Reininger/Leo de Wys, Inc.; 110 Bill Bachman/Leo de Wys, Inc.; 111 Bob Krist/Leo de Wys, Inc.; 112 Jean-Claude Lejeune/Stock Boston; 113 Ken O'Donoghue/©D.C. Heath; 114 *t* J. Sulley/The Image Works; *b*, 115 *l*, *tr* Marc Freedman; *br* Melissa Johnson. **Back cover** *t* Skjold/The Image Works; *c* John Owens/©D.C. Heath; *b* Sarah Putnam/©D.C. Heath.

Full Pronunciation Key for Footnoted Words

(Each pronunciation and definition is adapted from *Scott, Foresman Advanced Dictionary* by E.L. Thorndike and Clarence L. Barnhart.)

The pronunciation of each footnoted word is shown just after the word, in this way: **abbreviate** [ə brē′ vē āt]. The letters and signs used are pronounced as in the words below. The mark ′ is placed after a syllable with primary or heavy accent, as in the example above. The mark ′ after a syllable shows a secondary or lighter accent, as in **abbreviation** [ə brē′ vē ā′ shən].

Some words, taken from foreign languages, are spoken with sounds that do not otherwise occur in English. Symbols for these sounds are given in the key as "foreign sounds."

a	hat, cap	j	jam, enjoy	u	cup, butter
ā	age, face	k	kind, seek	ů	full, put
ä	father, far	l	land, coal	ü	rule, move
		m	me, am	v	very, save
b	bad, rob	n	no, in	w	will, woman
ch	child, much	ng	long, bring	y	young, yet
d	did, red			z	zero, breeze
		o	hot, rock	zh	measure, seizure
e	let, best	ō	open, go		
ē	equal, be	ô	order, all	ə represents:
ėr	term, learn	oi	oil, voice		a in about
		ou	house, out		e in taken
f	fat, if				i in pencil
g	go, bag	p	paper, cup		o in lemon
h	he, how	r	run, try		u in circus
		s	say, yes		
i	it, pin	sh	she, rush		
ī	ice, five	t	tell, it		
		th	thin, both		
		ŦH	then, smooth		

foreign sounds

Y as in French *du*. Pronounce (ē) with the lips rounded as for (ü).

à as in French *ami*. Pronounce (ä) with the lips spread and held tense.

œ as in French *peu*. Pronounce (ā) with the lips rounded as for (ō).

N as in French *bon*. The N is not pronounced, but shows that the vowel before it is nasal.

H as in German *ach*. Pronounce (k) without closing the breath passage.